I0531137

Tobit

and Ahikar

SCRIPTURAL RESEARCH INSTITUTE

Published by Digital Ink Productions, 2022

Copyright

Tobit and Ahikar

First edition. June 22, 2022

ISBN: 978-1-998288-17-5

The Words of Ahikar was written sometime before 500 BC. The Septuagint was translated into Greek at the Library of Alexandria between 250 and 132 BC.

These English translations were created by the Scriptural Research Institute in 2019 through 2022, primarily from the Codex Vaticanus, Codex Sinaiticus, and Greek translation of the Words of Ahikar, although the Codex Alexandrinus and Elephantine fragments of Ahikar were also used for reference. Additionally the Oxyrhynchus Papyri 1076 and 1584, and the Arabic, Armenian, and Old Slavonic translations of the Words of Ahikar were used for comparative analysis.

The image used for the cover is 'Tobias Heals his Blind Father' by Andrea Vaccaro, painted circa 1640.

Table of Contents

TABLE OF CONTENTS

TABLE OF CONTENTS

TABLE OF CONTENTS

Forward

The Words of Ahikar is the oldest surviving Israelite story, with known copies in Aramaic dating back to the 5th-century BC. As it has been translated into many languages over the past two and a half millennia, it now has several names and translations, including the Words of Ahiqar, the Story of Ahikar, and various variations of the name, including Achiacharos, from the Greek translation, Åhyqr from the Aramaic translation, Akyrios from the Old Slavonic translation, Ḥayqār from the Arabic translation, and Xikar from the Armenian translation. This translation uses the most common English variation of Ahikar, which is based on a transliteration of the oldest surviving Aramaic version of the name. The oldest fragments of this book found to date, were discovered in Elephantine, Egypt, and date to the 5th-century BC, making it a couple of centuries older than the oldest of the Dead Sea Scrolls.

While the story is set during the Assyrian Captivity of the Samaritans during the 7th century BC, it is generally accepted by scholars that the book was written in its current form in the 6th century BC, during the Babylonian Captivity of the Judahites. The primary reason for this dating is the repeated referenced to Bôlå (𐤍𐤋𐤏𐤉), which is generally accepted as a reference to the Neo-Babylonian god of the 6th century BC named Belu (-𐎗),

1

more commonly called Bel in English based on his appearance in the Septuagint's Book of Daniel, where he was called Bel (Βῆλ). This book also repeatedly refers to the Highest God, El Elyon, the ancient Canaanite and Israelite god from the Torah, however, does not mention Yahw, and therefore does not appear to have been written by a Judahite. As Tobit, one of the authors of the book of Tobit, claimed to be Ahikar's uncle, and a Naphtalite captive in Assyria, this indicates that Ahikar was viewed as being a Samaritan, and not a Judahite at the time that Tobit was written.

While Bôlå (𐡀𐡋𐡏𐡁) was the Aramaic translation of Belu (-𒂗), it was also the Aramaic translation of the Canaanite term Bôl (𐤋𐤏𐤁), more commonly spelled as Ba'al in English based on the Hebrew spelling of baal (בַּעַל), meaning 'lord,' or 'husband.' This means that if the text was written by a Samaritan during the Neo-Assyrian era, the term would have been a common Canaanite word used in Samaria for 'the Lord,' or at least a 'Lord.' According to all historical evidence, and the written evidence in the Septuagint and Masoretic Text, the Israelites at the time were using the term Ba'al to refer to several gods, including the god worshiped at the temples in Jerusalem and Samaria. Nevertheless, by the era of the oldest surviving fragments of Ahikar, the term does appear to have been interpreted as a reference to the Neo-Babylonian Bel, likely because the Israelites had stopped referring to their gods as Ba'al by that era.

Based on the Aramaic language Elephantine papyri, several Israelite deities were being worshiped at the Israelite Temple in Elephantine in the early-5th century BC, including Yahw, Anat, and Bethel. Bel does not appear to have been worshiped at the temple at the time, meaning that the Words of Ahikar would have already been viewed as a somewhat heretical historical text, much like the early Rabbinical view of Daniel, Proverbs, Ecclesiastes, Ezekiel, Job, and Enoch. Nevertheless, as Elephantine was the southern frontier of the Persian Empire at the time, and the Israelite community had existed there for centuries, at least since the Babylonian destruction of Judah, and probably since the Assyrian destruction of Samaria, the text would have held a historical significance to the Israelites living there, regardless of which gods were in the book. Whoever Bel started out as, he was later translated out of the text to make it compatible with Christianity and Islam, replaced with 'the Lord' in Christian translations, and Allah in Islamic translations.

It does not appear to have been considered a religious book by Judeans under Greek rule, or later when Judea became independent, and was not included in either the Septuagint or the Masoretic Text. Nevertheless, the author of the Book of Tobit, which is in the Septuagint, clearly viewed the Words of Ahikar as authentic, as his protagonist Tobit claimed that he was Ahikar's uncle, and both Ahikar and his nephew Nadan make a brief appearance in the book of Tobit at Tobit's son Tobiah's marriage feast in Nineveh. The Book of Tobit was likely written in the Median Empire, and carried into Judea by the priest Tobiah, who was listed as one of the leaders of the Israelites that returned to Judea after Cyrus II (the Great) released the Judahites when he conquered Babylon. Tobiah was later rejected from the Second Temple priesthood, as he could not prove his linage as a Levite, which is consistent with the Tobiah in the book of Tobit, who was a Naphtalite. A Tobian priesthood was later reported in Moab during Persian and Greek rule, suggesting the Book of Tobit was in use in the region. The Tobian Judahites (Τουβιανοὺς Ἰουδαίους) also appear to be the source of the Testaments of the Patriarchs, which for the most part were not accepted by the Sadducees and Pharisees, but were later adopted by the Christians, Sethians, and Gnostics.

The Book of Tobit appears to be from an older sect of Judaism, likely the one led by the 'false priest' Tobiah, who was expelled from the temple by Ezra when his genealogy could not be proven in 2nd Ezra. 2nd Ezra was the version of Ezra used by the Pharisee sect which emerged under the Hasmonean Dynasty, while Tobit, along with Enoch, Jubilees, and Job appears to have primarily been used by the Essenes sects.

In the mid-3rd century BC, King Ptolemy II Philadelphus of Egypt ordered a translation of the ancient Hebrew scriptures for the Library of Alexandria, which resulted in the creation of the Septuagint. It is generally accepted that there were several versions of the ancient Aramaic and Phoenician scriptures before the translation of the Septuagint, although the older books appear to have originated in Akkadian Cuneiform. The version of the book of Tobit found in the Codex Vaticanus and most surviving copies of the Septuagint, was translated into Greek from Aramaic and added to the Septuagint, likely before 200 BC when the Judean Revolt against the Ptolemys rule, resulted in most Jews and Samaritans fleeing from Egypt, either east into Judea, or south into Nubia. There is another version of the Book of Tobit found in the Codex Sinaiticus, which appears to be older than the version in the other codices, and not translated in the Ptolemy's Egypt, but somewhere in the Seleucid's Empire.

The Book of Tobit is generally viewed as fiction by most scholars for a variety of reasons. One major reason it is viewed as fiction is the presence of Tobit's cousin Ahikar, in both versions of the book, who is the protagonist of the Words of Ahikar, a book set in the same era, which is also considered fiction. It is quite clear from the text of Tobit, that it is the same Ahikar, and not just someone with the same name, as Ahikar's betrayal by his nephew is mentioned, which is part of the early section of Ahikar.

Nevertheless, both books, Tobit and Ahikar survive in various forms, meaning that they were edited multiple times before the versions that survive to the present were transcribed. The surviving copies of the Septuagint include two versions of the Book of Tobit, the more common form, found in the Codex Vaticanus, Codex Alexandrinus, and most other surviving copies of the Septuagint, and the less common version found in the Codex Sinaiticus. Additionally, fragments of Tobit found among the Oxyrhynchus Papyri don't match either the Vaticanus or Sinaiticus version of Tobit. The Oxyrhynchus Papyri are a collection of ancient texts found in southern Egypt dating to the Greek, Roman, and Byzantine eras of Egyptian history, approximately 300 BC to 640 AD. Among the Oxyrhynchus Papyri, two fragments of Tobit have been found, Papyrus 1594, dated to circa 275 AD, and Papyrus 1076, dated to circa 550 AD. Unfortunately, these fragments are extremely short, with only a few lines surviving from chapters 12 and 2 respectively.

The Oxyrhynchus Papyri fragments of Tobit are in Greek but do not match surviving versions found in the Septuagint codices, meaning there were no less than three Greek versions of Tobit in circulation by 350 AD, when the Codex Vaticanus and Codex Sinaiticus are dated to.

While the Greek translations must have originated in an Aramaic text, it does not survive to the present. Nor have any Hebrew translations been found, and it is possible it was not translated into Hebrew, as the text is contrary to the theology of Simon the Zealot, who originally ordered the creation of the Hebrew translations of the ancient Israelite scriptures. The Peshitta does include a version of Tobit that may have been translated directly from the Aramaic source, however, western scholarship leans towards it having been translated from the Septuagint.

The differences between the Vaticanus and Sinaiticus versions of Tobit are too extensive to treat the books as the same book, however, their story is essentially the same. The two books must have had a common source, however, the Sinaiticus' version is over 20% longer than the Vaticanus' version, and appears to be an older version of Tobit. One of the reasons that the Book of Tobit is interpreted as fiction, is the existence of historical errors and anachronisms found in the Vaticanus version, which includes the Babylonian king Nebuchadnezzar (Ναβουχοδονοσορ) and the Persian king Xerxes (Ασυηρος) jointly destroying Nineveh, the capital of the Assyrian Empire. Nineveh was sacked by Babylonian King

Nabopolassar in 612 BC, along with Median and Persian allies, led by the Median King Cyaxares, who then integrated the city into his Median Empire. Nabopolassar's son Nebuchadnezzar, who assumed the throne in 605 BC, finally conquered the remnants of the Assyrian forces in Syria at the Battle of Carchemish that same year, however, he did not attack or destroy Nineveh. Meanwhile, the name Ahasuerus (Ασυηρος) was the Aramaic name of Xerxes, the Persian king who ruled between 486 and 465 BC.

These anachronisms are not found in the Codex Sinaiticus' version, which does not mention either king, but gives credit to King Achiacharos (Αχιαχαρος) of Media, which is likely an attempt to transliterate the Median name of King Cyaxares into Aramaic. Cyaxares's Median name was Uvaxshtra (𐎢𐎺𐎧𐏁𐎫𐎼), however, it was transliterated several ways into the languages and scripts of the day, including the Neo-Babylonian Úaksatar (𒌑𒀝𒊓𒋻), the Elamite Makiišturri (𒈠𒆠𒅖𒌅𒊑), the Phrygian Ksuwaksaros (ΚΣΟϜΑΨΣΡΟΣ), and the Greek Cyaxares (Κυαξάρης) from which the modern English name is derived. The Sinaiticus version of Tobit describes King Achiacharos as conquering Nineveh and integrating it into his Median Kingdom, which, was done by King Cyaxares according to the Median, Persian, Babylonian, Egyptian, and Greek records from the era, and so, even if the origin of the name is disputed, the person described is King Cyaxares. There are several differences between the Vaticanus and Sinaiticus versions that point to the Sinaiticus version being older, and that point to the Vaticanus version being a later translation created in Alexandria, likely from an Aramaic early-Jewish redaction of the original Aramaic version.

Tobit's book was largely about his son Tobiah's journey to Ecbatana, the capital of the kingdom of Media, in the territory of northern modern Iran. The journey is set circa 673 BC, during the reign of King Esarhaddon of Assyria. After inheriting the Assyrian throne in 681 BC, when two of his brothers had killed his father Sennacherib, Esarhaddon spent several years suppressing rebellions across his empire, that some historians believe were in support of his older brother Arda-Mulissu, who had led the conspiracy to kill their father, and then fled to Urartu after a six-week civil war against Esarhaddon for the throne. These campaigns across the empire led to additional campaigns into the Caucasus Mountains, Anatolia, and the Arabian Peninsula, as well as Media, where several tribes of Medes were subjugated into the empire. Esarhaddon's conquests culminated in the conquest of Egypt in 671 BC, however, he could not capture Kush itself, which had been ruling Egypt for centuries by the time the Assyrians captured it.

It is unclear how much control thee Assyrians exercised over Media, as several tribes of Medes did agree to pay tribute after the Assyrians defeated the Median chiefs Eparna and Shidirparna circa 675 BC, however, a chief the Assyrians called Kashtariti (𒁹𒅗𒀸𒋫𒊑𒋾), which the Old Persian records later transliterated as Xshathrita (𐎧𐏁𐎰𐎼𐎡𐎫) continued to attack the Assyrians throughout Esarhaddon's reign. It has been theorized that this was the legendary King Phraortes (𐎳𐎼𐎺𐎼𐎫𐎡𐏁), which according to Old Persian records, started a war against the Assyrians, and was ultimately killed by Esarhaddon's heir Ashurbanipal. It is also possible that he was one of many Median chiefs that did not recognize the authority of the Assyrians, as the surviving records indicated the region swung rapidly back and forth between Assyrian control and Median rebellion.

Tobiah's traveling companion to Ecbatana was the angel Raphael, who disguised himself as a Naphtalite to help Tobiah marry his cousin, who was possessed by an ancient Zoroastrian demon. After returning from Ecbatana, Raphael healed Tobit, who had lost his sight eight years earlier. The story continues after Tobit died, with Tobiah moving to Ecbatana, which implies he continued writing his father's book. It is unclear how or when the book was carried from Media to Judea and Egypt, however, this likely happened during the

Persian era, when all the lands were under the same empire.

The Words of Ahikar is not considered to be a true historical story by any modern academics or theologians. It is universally considered to be a work of fiction for several reasons, not the least of which are the boys flying on the back of trained eagles. Another reason that the work is not considered historical, is that the Assyrian kings are not mentioned in the correct order, as King Esarhaddon was actually Sennacherib's son, not his father. Both Kings are well known from the historical records of the Assyrians, Babylonians, and Egyptians. Moreover, Esarhaddon and his son Ashurbanipal liberated Egypt from Kushite rule, and established the vassal state of Egypt which ultimately became independent again when the Neo-Assyrian Empire fell. During the time of Sennacherib, Egypt was still under the control of Kush, and there was no Pharaoh for Ahikar to visit.

The book also refers to a King of Persia, a century before there was a Kingdom of Persia, and is therefore generally dismissed as a work of historical-fiction. Nevertheless, the book of Tobit records that Ahikar was sent to Elam as an envoy, not Persia. As the Persians settled in the land of Elam after King Ashurbanipal destroyed Elam in the mid-7th century BC, the name Persia would have been the contemporary geographical term when the Aramaic translation was made, and not the original term. In any event, the author of Tobit must have had a copy of Ahikar that used the name Elam instead of Persia, or his reference to Ahikar going to Elam makes no sense. As Ahikar, Tobit, and Tobiah are all reported as living in Nineveh under the reign of Esarhaddon, and both Tobit and Ahikar are reported to have worked in his court, they would have almost certainly written their books in Neo-Assyrian Cuneiform. Tobiah, Tobit's son added to Tobit's writing after he moved to Media, which would have probably also have been in Neo-Assyrian, and the earliest Aramaic translation of Tobit was probably not made until the Persian era, when the Median King Cyaxares (Αχιαχαρος) was replaced with the Babylonian king Nebuchadnezzar (Ναβουχοδονοσορ) and the Persian king Xerxes (Ασυηρος). This indicates that the Neo-Assyrian original of Ahikar used the name Elam, not Persia, and therefore is not evidence of the book being written later, during the Persian era.

Regardless of the obvious fictional additions to the text, there is some evidence supporting the existence of Ahikar as a historical person. A cuneiform text discovered in the ruins of Uruk in southern Iraq, mentions that Aḫuúkaari (𒈾𒆠𒅁𒍣𒀭𒌋) was the Akkadian name of the sage Aba Enlil Dari (𒀀𒁀𒂗𒆤𒁕𒌋) during the reign of the Assyrian King Esarhaddon. This correlates with the opening of Ahikar, where King Sennacherib claims that Ahikar had served his father Esarhaddon, unfortunately, Esarhaddon was actually Sennacherib's son, not his father. Therefore, one of the names of the kings must have been replaced at some point, either the elder king, called Esarhaddon in the surviving text, or the younger king, called Sennacherib in the text.

The historical succession of Assyrian kings who may have been in the original text were Sargon II, Sennacherib, Esarhaddon, and Ashurbanipal. Sargon II was the king that fought the Levantine Wars, and in the process destroyed Samaria. The conquest of Samaria took three years, and was finally completed in the first year of his successor Sennacherib. During the war, Sargon reported deporting 27,280 Samaritans, who were resettled in other regions of his empire. Sennacherib reported deporting more in the aftermath of the war. It seems unlikely that Ahikar could have worked for Sargon II, before or during the Levantine Wars, as he was clearly some kind of Canaanite, and probably a Samaritan as Tobit reported. Therefore, it is probable that the elder king was named Esarhaddon, and the younger king was Ashurbanipal, the same king as in the Book of Tobit.

King Sennacherib continued Sargon's campaigns in Levant, including the siege of Jerusalem, and it seems unlikely that Ahikar would have been sent to the Empire of Kush to represent Assyrian interests while the Assyrians were at war against his own people, and the Kushites were backing them. Nevertheless,

Sennacherib is a much more famous king in the Israelite scriptures compared to Ashurbanipal, who existed peacefully with his vassal King Manasseh of Judah, and was hardly mentioned. This may be the reason he was later replaced by Sennacherib, like the other kings who were replaced by more famous kings in the various versions of the books of Tobit, Judith, and Esther.

King Esarhaddon, the elder king in Akihar, and the king he served according to the tablet found in Uruk, did not fight any recorded wars against Judah, as King Manasseh appears to have been a firm Assyrian-ally throughout his reign. Esarhaddon did fight a series of wars in the north, against the kingdom of Urartu in the Armenian highlands, and the Cimmerians from Ukraine, who launched a massive invasion of the western region of the Assyrian empire after defeating the kingdoms of western Anatolia. After his victory in the north, he turned his attention to the south and launched a massive invasion of the Kushite Empire, sacking northern Egypt in 671 BC. In 669 BC he launched another campaign into Kush, attempting to reach southern Egypt, but died en route to Egypt. It is unclear if he died of natural causes or was assassinated, as he did have poor health, and there were several assassination plots that were foiled in the latter years of his life.

King Ashurbanipal continued his father's campaigns in Egypt in 667 BC, and managed to capture Thebes in southern Egypt, which they reorganized into a Persian tributary, placing King Necho I on the throne of Egypt, before withdrawing to Assyria, in 664 BC. This withdrawal was immediately followed by the king of Kush invading Egypt, and killing Necho I. The Assyrians returned in force, and drove the Kushites from Egypt, placing Necho I's heir Psamtik I on the throne. This occupation of Thebes was recorded as the 'Sack of Thebes,' in the Assyrian and Israelite records. The Assyrians are believed to have taken over 75 tons of gold from Thebes, most of which had been coating the exterior of statues and obelisks. Both the Judahite prophet Isaiah, and the Babylonian prophet Nahum commented on this, with Nahum predicting that Assyria would one day suffer the same fate. At the time, Babylonia was quasi-independent under the rule of Ashurbanipal's elder brother Shamash-shum-ukin, and so criticism of Assyria appears to have been tolerated.

The exact level of Babylonian independence at the time is unclear, however, it appears that Esarhaddon placed his sons on the thrones of the two kingdoms of Assyria and Babylon in order to avoid a civil war after he died. Ashurbanipal was the more militant, and placed on the throne of Assyria to continue the wars against Egypt and Urartu, while Shamash-shum-ukin was placed on the throne of Babylon to continue rebuilding the nation that had been largely destroyed when the

Assyrian king Tiglath-Pileser had captured it around a century earlier. Esarhaddon had invested significantly in rebuilding the land, and Shamash-shum-ukin continued his work for decades before openly declaring war against his brother Ashurbanipal who had tried to incorporate Babylonia into the Assyrian Empire. As the Assyrians ultimately won the war, this was recorded as a civil war in the Assyrian records, however, Babylonia appears to have been a functionally independent closely allied state under the rule of Shamash-shum-ukin, with its own military and foreign relations.

Nahum's prophecy against Assyria is referenced in the Codex Sinaiticus' version of Tobit, however, it is substituted by Jonah's prophecy against Assyria in the Codex Vaticanus' version of Tobit. While the conflicting versions of Tobit may not be the best historical evidence for the existence of Ahikar, it is worth noting that Ahikar and his nephew Nadan are mentioned as attending Tobiah's wedding in Nineveh during the reign of Esarhaddon, which would have to have been before Nadan betrayed Ahikar. This, combined with the claim that Ahikar was the son of Tobit's brother Anael, and that they both served Esarhaddon, indicate that at least the author of Tobit believed that Ahikar served Esarhaddon and Ashurbanipal, not Sargon and Sennacherib.

The references to Bel in the oldest surviving copies of Ahikar indicate that the Aramaic translation was made in the Neo-Babylonian Empire, which explains why the name of Ashurbanipal would have been replaced, as he fought a massive war against Babylonia, and reoccupied it after defeating his brother Shamash-shum-ukin. No book about someone serving Ashurbanipal would have been popular in the Neo-Babylonian empire, and owning one could have been viewed as treason in and of itself after Babylon finally threw off the shackles of Assyria.

There are few other historic references to someone who may have been Ahikar, however, these references are generally centuries later, and may simply be based on people reading copies of the Words of Ahikar. In the 5th-century BC, the Greek historian Herodotus mentioned a similar character named Croesus (Κροῖσος), however, placed the wise sage in the court of the Persian King Cyrus I, around 50 years after the events described int the Words of Ahikar. Some modern historians believe that Croesus is a corruption of the Greek version of Akihar's name: Achiacharos (Αχιαχαρος), making Herodotus' Croesus another version of the Ahikar story, however, the name Croesus is more commonly viewed as being derived from the Lydian name Krowiśaś (𐤓𐤀𐤛𐤘𐤅𐤖𐤀), making any connection between Ahikar and Croesus speculative. If Ahikar did serve in the court of Esarhaddon, which all copies of

Ahikar and Tobit agree on, then he would have been an adult before Esarhaddon's death in 705 BC, while King Cyrus I did not become king of Persia until 600 BC, making this seem to be an impossibility. In the 1st-century BC, the Greek historian Strabo mentioned an ancient eastern sage named Achaicarus (Αχαικαρος), who many believe was a reference to Ahikar, however, Strabo could have simply read a copy of the Words of Ahikar.

The Words of Ahikar includes many similar sayings to the Septuagint's Book of Proverbs, which many interpret as being an Judahite influence, however, the Book of Proverbs could have also been used by Samaritans at the time. Other than the existence of El Elyon (the Highest God) there does not seem to be any common element with the Torah. There is no mention of Abraham, Isaac, Jacob, Moses, Aaron, or Joshua, and therefore this book could be interpreted as a Canaanite work, and not Israelite at all, meaning neither Jewish nor Samaritan, however, it is generally assumed by academics to be Israelite. The surviving full copies in Greek, Armenian, and Arabic, all show signs of later Christian or Islamic editors, and therefore, it is unclear who wrote the book, a Canaanite or an Israelite, however, it does mention Bel by name, which is taken as proof that it was either written or edited in the Neo-Babylonian Empire, and it does mention El Elyon by name, which is taken as proof it is Israelite. This is in and of itself not conclusive, as the Arameans in northern Canaan are recorded as worshiping a version of El Elyon, called ȧl wȧlyn (𐤉𐤏𐤋𐤉𐤍 𐤋𐤍), in the Sfire Treaties of the mid 8th-century BC.

Unfortunately, while the fragments found in Elephantine do allow us to restore the name Bel to the text, which was changed to either 'Lord' (κύριος), or Allah (الله) in surviving copies, the fragments do not indicate who the god was before the Neo-Babylonian Aramaic translation. Moreover as all surviving translations appear to be based on an Aramaic translation made in the Neo-Babylonian era, they all also include the anachronisms that the Aramaic translator introduced when he obfuscated King Ashurbanipal, creating a somewhat nonsensical text from the historical perspective. Therefore two versions are included in this translation. The first is a translation of the Words of Ahikar, reconstructed primarily from the Greek version, with comparisons to the Aramaic fragments, as well as the Arabic, Armenian, and Old Slavonic translations. The second version is a historical restoration that uses the name Ashurbanipal instead of Sennacherib, and corrects other anachronisms as much as possible. In both versions there are still references to unknown places and peoples, however, after 2700 years, it does seem likely that there would be.

Tobit (Vaticanus): Chapter 1

The book of the words of Tobit,[1] son of Tobiel, son of Ananiel, son of Aduel, son of Gabael of the descendants of Asahel, of the tribe of Naphtali, who in the time of King Sargon II[2] of the Assyrians was led captive out of Tishbe,[3] which is to the right of Kadesh of Naphtali in Galilee near Asher.

I, Tobit, have followed all the days of my life in the ways of truth and justice, and I was very charitable to my brothers from my nation, who came with me to Nineveh in the land of the Assyrians. When I was still young in my own country of Israel, all of my father's tribe of Naphtali abandoned the temple in Jerusalem,[4] which was chosen out of all the tribes of Israel that all the tribes should sacrifice there, where the temple and tabernacle[5] of the Highest[6] was consecrated and built for all ages.

All the tribes which joined together sacrificed to Ba'al the calf,[7] including the house of Naphtali my father Naphtali.

I regularly went by myself to Jerusalem at the feasts, as it was ordained to all Israel by an eternal decree, having the tithe of the animals and the first-born, with that which was first cut, and I gave them to the priests, the sons of Aaron, the firstborns for the altar, and the tithe I gave to the Levites who served in Jerusalem. A second tenth I would spend on everything in Jerusalem, each year. The third amount I gave as it was my duty, as Debora my father's mother had commanded me, because I was left an orphan by my father.

When I had come to the age of a man, I married my relative Hannah, and through her, I became the father of Tobiah. When we were taken away captives to Nineveh, all my brothers and those that were of my families ate the food of the nations, but I kept myself from eating it because I remembered God with all my heart. The Highest gave me grace and favor before Sargon II, so that I became the purchaser of his provisions. I went into Media,[8] and once left in trust with Gabael, the brother of Gabri, in the Median city of Ray[9] ten talents of silver.

When Sargon II was dead, Sennacherib[10] his son reigned in his place, whose land was troubled and I could not go into Media. In the time of Sargon, I was very charitable to my brothers and gave my bread to the hungry, my clothes to the naked, and if I saw any of my nation dead, or thrown out of the walls of Nineveh, I buried him. If King Sennacherib killed any, when he came back from Judea, I buried them privately, for in his anger he killed many, but the bodies were not found when they were searched for by the king.

When one of the Ninevites went and complained about me to the king, that I buried them, I hid, knowing that I was being searched for, to be put to death, and I ran away in fear. Then, all my goods were seized and there was nothing left to me, other than my wife Hannah and my son Tobiah. Less than fifty days passed, before two of his sons killed him,[11] and they fled into the mountains of Urartu,[12] and Esarhaddon[13] his son reigned in his place, who appointed over his father's accounts, and over all his affairs, Ahikar[14] my brother Anael's son. Ahikar asked about me, and I returned to Nineveh. Ahikar was cup-bearer, and keeper of the signet, and steward, and overseer of the accounts, and Esarhaddon appointed him second to himself, and he was my nephew.

Tobit (Vaticanus): Chapter 1 Notes

1) Codex Vaticanus: Tôbit (ⲦⲱⲂⲉⲓⲦ)

- Codex Sinaiticus: Tôbith (ⲦⲱⲂⲉⲓⲑ)

- Septuagint manuscript 106: Tôbit (Τωβιτ)

- Septuagint manuscript 248: Tôbêt (Τωβητ)

- Septuagint manuscript 392: Tôbid (Τωβειδ)

The names in the various manuscripts of the book of Tobit/Tobith/Tobid are not standardized, including the names of the book itself. This indicates three or more separate translations into Greek, as no one would have a reason to change the names if redacting one to make the other. The more common English name 'Tobit' is used in this translation.

2) Codex Vaticanus: Enemessarou (ⲉⲛⲉⲙⲉⲥⲥⲁⲣⲟⲩ)

- Septuagint ms. 46: Ennemesarou (Εννεμεσαρου)

- Septuagint ms. 71: Enemesarou (Ενεμεσαρου)

- Septuagint ms. 318: Enaimesarou (Εναιμεσαρου)

- Septuagint ms 122: Enemesarrou (Ενεμεσαρρου)

- Septuagint ms. 249: Enemassarou (Ενεμασσαρου)

- Septuagint ms. 107: Nemessarou (Νεμεσσαρου)

- Sahidic manuscripts: Namessaros (Ναⲙⲉⲥⲥⲁⲣⲟⲥ)

Based on the rest of the book this must be a reference to Sargon II, King of Assyria between 722 and 705 BC. The name is often mistranslated as Shalmaneser, however, Enemessarou's son is later identified as Sennacherib, who was Sargon II's son. Shalmaneser was recorded in the books of the Kingdoms (Masoretic Kings), as having conquered Samaria, however, while Shalmaneser V's armies did besiege Samaria for three years, he died before Samaria surrendered, and when they surrendered, it was to Sargon II, Shalmaneser V's heir, who recorded in his records that he deported 27,920 Samaritans to Assyria.

This appears to have been an Aramaic translation of his Assyrian name Šarru-kīnum (𒈗𒁺𒆕𒅕), with the Assyrian terms inverted to Kīnum-šarru. His name is believed to translate as approximately as 'king who is legitimate,' suggesting the Aramaic translator interpreted then name as 'legitimate king,' and was not basing the reference on a historic record of the king, after his throne name had become standardized, but lived in the era of Sargon II.

Assuming this is a reference to Sargon, which it appears to be, it is notable that in the Book of Isaiah, the name Šarru-kīnum is rendered as Sargôn (סַרְגוֹן), meaning that the Book of Tobit is not dependent on Isaiah, and was likely translated into Aramaic by someone who had not read Isaiah. This supports the author's claims to be a Samaritan living in Assyria, and the dating of the text to the era of the Assyrian Empire. The Hebrew-derived name 'Sargon' is used in this translation, as it is more common in modern English.

3) Codex Vaticanus: Tishbes (ΘΙϹΒΗϹ)

• Codex Alexandrinus: Thêbês (ΘΗΒΗϹ)

• Peshitta: Ṭḥbḥš (ܬܚܒܚܫ). Translation: Thebes

• Codex Corbeiensis (VL 150): Bibel

• Codex Sangermanensis 4 (VL 7): Viel

• Codex Complutensis 1 (VL 109): Biel

• Codex Monacensis (VL 130): Cibiel

TOBIT (VATICANUS): CHAPTER 1 NOTES

- Codex Bobbiensis (VL 135): Sibiel

- Ge'ez ms.: Thêbêsə (ﾒﾊﾊﾊ). Translation: Thebes

The Vaticanus and Sinaiticus manuscripts agree that is was the accepted Greek translation of the town called Tishbe (תִּשְׁבֵּ) in Hebrew, however, not all biblical scholars agree that there was a town called Tishbe in the Masoretic Texts. The issue revolves around the meaning of the word tishbi (תִּשְׁבִּי), which could simply be interpreted as 'resident,' however, was traditionally interpreted as Tishbite, meaning someone from Tishbe. The prophet Elijah was recorded as being a Tishbite, or maybe a 'resident,' in the Masoretic Kings (3rd Kingdoms) chapter 17. The Septuagint's translation is clearer, where he is recorded as being a Tishbite from Tishbe (Θεσβίτης ἐκ Θεσβων), and so this translation accepts the traditional interpretation of the name Tishbe. It is significant though, that Elijah was closely connected with the Assyrian Samaritans on the Khabur River, where he saw the cherubs and the flying chariot in the cloud of fire and lightning. If he was from the same town as those relocated by Sargon II, it would make sense for him to visit them, as they would have been his cousins.

A large number of Greek, Latin, Syriac, and Ge'ez manuscripts deviate on this name, with the largest alternate reading being Thebes. It is unclear if this was intended to represent Thebes in Egypt, or Greece, or another town in the mind of the translator. Thebes was a city in Greece at the time, however, the city later renamed Thebes in Egypt, was still known as was still known as Wôst (ⲓ).

The name Thêbês (ⲐⲎⲂⲎⲤ) in the Codex Vaticanus, and Thebes (ⲐⲉⲂⲉⲤ) in the Codex Alexandrinus, was also used as a translation for a name of a town in Canaan in the book of Judges chapter 9. The town's name is rendered as Tbs (תבץ) in the Aleppo Codex, and Têbês (תֵּבֵץ) in the Leningrad Codex, and is generally accepted as

26

being Tubas (طوباس) in the northern area of the modern Palestinian West Bank. As this is in the region where Tishbe (תִּשְׁבִּ) was supposed to have been located, it is possible that both names refer to the same town.

4) Codex Vaticanus: oecou Ierosolymôn (ΟΙΚΟΥΙΕΡΟCΟΛΥΜΩ). Translation: house (or temple) in Jerusalem

• Codex Sinaiticus: Ierousalêm poleôs (ΙΕΡΟΥCΑΛΗΜ ΠΟΛΕΩC). Translation: Jerusalem town

5) Codex Vaticanus: catascênôseôs (ΚΑΤΑCΚΗΝΩCΕΩC). Translation: camping place

This is most likely an attempt to translate 'tabernacle' into Greek via Aramaic, and so the more common term is used in this translation.

6) Codex Vaticanus: ypsístou (ΥΨΙCΤΟΥ). Translation: highest

The Highest is a reference to God, or a god, found in many ancient religions in the region. According to the Torah, the ancient people of Salem worshiped El Elyon, which translates as Highest God when Abraham passed through the regions. The term Highest repeats through other early Jewish and Samaritan texts.

7) The codices tell essentially the same story, however, the Codex Vaticanus version appears to be a Jewish redaction of the Codex Sinaiticus version. The setting of the event is during the life of Jeroboam II, the king of Samaria between circa 768 and 746 BC. His kingdom briefly conquered the Arameans of Damascus and Hama, creating the largest Israelite kingdom since the era of King

David, and the largest that is known archaeologically, as evidence of the earlier United Kingdom of Israel has yet to be found. He was recorded as building shrines with icons of the calf-god in them, which outraged the prophets at the time, including Amos. The Vaticanus's reference to the Ba'al calf is anachronistic, as the god Ba'al Hadad was not depicted as a calf, although he was depicted as having horns, like many Middle-eastern gods. Based on the archaeological evidence, such as the potshards discovered at Khirbet el-Kom and Kuntillet Ajrud, the calf-god worshiped in Samaria circa 800 BC was Yahweh.

8) Codex Vaticanus: Midian (ΜΗΔΙΑΝ)

Media was the name of the land of the Medes, and ancient Iranian people who lived in northern Iran before the rise of the Persian Empire. The Medians were the allies of the Babylonians that jointly conquered the Assyrian Empire, a few decades after the story is set.

9) Codex Vaticanus: Ragoes (ΡΑΓΟΙC)

- Septuagint manuscript 318: Ragoê (Ραγοη)

- Septuagint manuscript 670: Raga (Ραγα)

- Septuagint manuscript 319: Rassois (Ρασσοις)

- Septuagint manuscript 64: Agrois (Αγροις)

This is accepted as the Greek name of Ray (ری), an ancient city near Tehran in Iran. It is regarded as the oldest continuously inhabited city in Tehran Province, dating back to the Median Empire. The Greek name used in this book is likely a transliteration of the Aramaic name from the era, itself transliterated from the Assyrian name Raga (𒀭𒆜𒅖𒐏𒁹). The older Elamite name was

Rakkaan (𒊏𒅗𒀭), while the later Old Persian name was Ragae (𐎼𐎥𐎠).

10) Codex Vaticanus: Sennachirim (ϹΕΝΝΑΧΗΡΙΜ)

- Codex Venetus (LXX V): Chirim (ΧΕΙΡΕΙΜ)
- Septuagint manuscript 74: Rim (Ριμ)
- Septuagint manuscript 314: Chirim (Χιριμ)
- Septuagint ms. 98: Senachrim (Σεναχρειμ)
- Septuagint ms. 318: Senachirim (Σεναχειρειμ)
- Septuagint ms. 106: Senachirim (Σεναχιρειμ)
- Septuagint ms. 130: Senachrim (Σεναχριμ)
- Septuagint ms. 71: Senachirim (Σεναχειριμ)
- Septuagint ms. 76: Senachirim (Σεναχιριμ)
- Septuagint ms. 402: Senacherim (Σεναχερειμ)
- Septuagint ms. 126: Senachechrim (Σεναχεχριμ)
- Septuagint ms. 319: Senachri (Σεναχρι)
- Septuagint ms. 46: Sennachrib (Σενναχρειβ)
- Septuagint ms. 44: Naxim (Ναχιμ)
- Sahidic manuscripts: Senakherim (Ⲥⲉⲛⲁⲭⲉⲣⲓⲙ)

King Sennacherib was the king of the Assyrian Empire between 705 and 681 BC. His reign was spent fighting a series of insurrections in Babylonia and Canaan. He also launched a punitive invasion of Elam, that virtually wiped out the nation. His campaigns in Canaan included laying siege to Jerusalem, which had previously been allied to Assyria.

11) This was the year 681 BC, when Sennacherib was killed by his sons Arda-Mulissu and Nabu-shar-usur. This is calculated by Assyriologists as having taken place on 20 October, meaning Tobit would have gone into hiding sometime in early September.

12) Codex Vaticanus: Ararath (ⲀⲢⲀⲢⲀⲐ)

• Codex Sinaiticus: Ararat (ⲀⲢⲀⲢⲀⲦ)

• Sahidic manuscripts: Ararad (ⲁⲣⲁⲣⲁⲇ)

The Assyrian records record the princes as retreating to the Kingdom of ᵏᵘʳUrartu (𒆳𒌑𒊏𒀳) in the Armenian Highlands. The name of this country was recorded as Ararat (אֲרָרָט) in Hebrew, and Urartu (Ուրարտու) in Armenian. The Greek name is a transliteration of the Hebrew name, however, the more common historical name of Urartu is used in this translation.

13) Codex Vaticanus: Sacherdonos (ⲤⲀⲬⲈⲢⲆⲞⲚⲞⲤ)

• Codex Alexandrinus: Sacherdan (ⲤⲀⲬⲈⲢⲆⲀⲚ)

• Codex Venetus: Nacherdonos (ⲚⲀⲬⲈⲢⲆⲞⲚⲞⲤ)

• Septuagint ms. 74: Sacherdônos (Σαχερδωνος)

• Septuagint ms. 314: Sacherdon (Σαχερδον)

• Septuagint ms. 538: Sacherdôn (Σαχερδων)

• Septuagint ms. 64: Sarchedonos (Σαρχεδονοσ)

• Septuagint ms. 46: Sachedôr (Σαχεδωρ)

• Septuagint ms. 248: Acherdonos (Αχερδονος)

• Septuagint ms. 98: Achirdônos (Αχειρδωνος)

• Septuagint ms. 542: Nachordanos (Ναχορδανος)

- Sahidic manuscripts: Sakherdônias (CⲁxepⲁⲱNιⲁc)
- Armenian Bible: Asordan (Ասորդաւ)
- Codex Corbeiensis (VL 150): Archedonassar
- Codex Monacensis (VL 130): Arcedonossar
- Codex Bobbiensis (VL 135): Nachoda
- Codex Complutensis 1 (VL 109): Natordan

Esarhaddon is the more common name of King Aššur-Aḫa-Iddina, Sennacherib's youngest son and heir. The name Esarhaddon is derived from the Latin Hazor Haddan, which was in turn derived from the Greek Asarchaddon (Ασαρχαδδων), which was used in direct translations from Assyrian texts. Sacherdonos (Σαχερδονος) appears to be a Greek transliteration of the Aramaic version of his name.

14) Codex Vaticanus: Achiacharon (ⲀxιⲀxⲀpⲟN)

- Codex Sinaiticus: Achicharon (ⲀxιxⲀpⲟN)
- Septuagint ms. 107: Achiachar (Ⲁxιⲁxⲁp)
- Vetus Latina manuscripts: Achicarum

This name is generally translated as Ahikar, the famous, possibly fictional hero of the Words of Ahikar, the oldest known Jewish or Samaritan text to survive intact to the present. The oldest copy found to date is from around 500 BC, a couple of centuries older than the oldest of the Dead Sea Scrolls. Tobit does allude to the story of Ahikar's betrayal by his nephew, which is found in the Words of Ahikar, and it is accepted that this was a reference to that Ahikar, however, both stories are also regarded as fiction by most scholars, and so the authors may have been the same person.

It is also possible that both books began as historical texts that then became fictionalized, however, if additional elements were added, they must have been added to the Words of Ahikar before the oldest surviving copy, from circa 500 BC. As both Ahikar and Tobit are reported to have lived circa 700 BC, this is not a great deal of time for the books to have been altered, however, as all books were copied by hand at the time, it is possible that the scribes felt a more fantastic version of the tales of these two men's lives would sell better.

Tobit (Vaticanus): Chapter 2

When I returned home again, my wife Hannah was restored to me, along with my son Tobiah. At the feast of Pentecost, which is the holy feast of the seven weeks, there was a good dinner prepared for me, in which I sat down to eat. When I saw the abundance of food, I said to my son, "Go and bring whatever poor man you find from among our brothers, who worships the Lord,[1] and I'll wait for you."

But when he returned he said, "Father, one of our nation is strangled, and is throw out in the marketplace."

Then, before I had tasted any of the food, I got up and took him up into a room to wait until the sun went down. Then I returned, and washed myself, and ate my food in hunger, remembering the prophecy of Amos,[2] when he said, 'Your feasts will be turned into mourning, and all your happiness into sadness.' I wept, and after the sun set, I went and dug a grave and buried him.

My neighbors mocked me, and said, "This man is not afraid to be put to death over this matter, he who ran away. Look, he buries the dead again."

The same night I returned from the burial, I slept by the wall of my courtyard, as I was unclean. My face was uncovered, and I did not know that there were sparrows in the wall, and while my eyes were open, the sparrows dropped warm dung into my eyes. A white film came into my eyes, and I went to the physicians, but they could not help me. However, Ahikar took care of me, until he went to Elam.[3]

My wife Hannah took women's work. Once, when she had sent them home to the owners, they paid her wages and also gave her a goat. When it was in my house and began to bleat, I demanded of her, "Where did this goat come from? Is it stolen? Return it to the owners, for it is not lawful to eat anything that is stolen."

But she replied to me, "It was given as a gift in addition to my wages."

I did not believe her and commanded her to return it to its owners, and I was angry with her, but she replied to me, "Where are your charitable works and your righteous deeds? Look, are all your works known?"

Tobit (Vaticanus): Chapter 2 Notes

1) Codex Vaticanus: cyriou (ΚΥΡΙΟΥ). Translation: lord (or main, chief, dominant, master)

- Septuagint ms. 249: Cyriô (Κυριω). Translation: lord (or main, chief, dominant, master)

In some early fragments of the Septuagint, the name Iaw (Ιαω), Greek for Yahweh, survives instead of the term Lord (Κυρίου), however, there is no surviving text of Tobit that includes the name, and based on Tobit's referring to the Baʿal calf, it seems unlikely he worshiped Yahweh, or that the name would have been in his writing.

2) The Prophet Amos was active in Samaria and Judah between 760 and 755 BC, and is believed to have died in 745 BC, about 66 years before this event.

3) Codex Vaticanus: Ellymaeda (ЄΛΛΥΜΑΙΔΑ)

- Codex Sinaiticus: Elymaeda (ЄΛΥΜΑΙΔΑ)

- Septuagint ms. 107: Elimaeda (Ελιμαιδα)

- Septuagint ms. 98: Eloemaeda (Ελοιμαιδα)

- Septuagint ms. 71: Elemaeda (Ελεμαιδα)

- Septuagint ms. 126: Lymaeda (Λυμαιδα)

- Codex Corbeiensis (VL 150): Limaidam

- Codex Monacensis (VL 130): Lymaidem

Haltamti (𒀪𒈙𒋼𒅗𒉌) was a major nation in southern modern Iran, until it was virtually destroyed by the kings of Assyria in the

7th-century BC. The Babylonian name of the land was Elamma[ki] (𒀲𒈠𒆠), which was adopted into Hebrew as Elam (עֵילָם) and Greek as Elám (Ελάμ), ultimately resulting in the modern English name Elam. The conflict in question is likely the events near the beginning of Esarhaddon's rule, when an ethnically Elamite Assyrian governor named Nabu-zer-kitti-lišir in southern Babylonia revolted against Assyrian rule and besieged Ur. Esarhaddon's army defeated Nabu-zer-kitti-lišir, and he fled to Elam, where he was ultimately captured and executed.

Tobit (Vaticanus): Chapter 3

I began to cry, and in my grief prayed, "Sydyk exists! Lord, all your works and all your ways are mercy and truth, and you judge truly and justly forever. Remember me! See me, but don't punish me for my sins and ignorance, and the sins of my fathers, who have sinned before you. They did not obey your commandments, and therefore you have given us as a plunder, and into captivity, and to death, and as an example of reproach to all the nations among whom we are dispersed."

"Now, your judgments are many and true. Deal with me according to my sins and my fore-fathers' because we have not kept your commandments, nor have walked honestly before you. Now, therefore, deal with me as seems best to you, and command my spirit to be taken from me, that I may be dissolved, and become dirt, for it is preferable for me to die rather than to live, because I have heard false insults, and have much sorrow. Command therefore that I may now be delivered out of this distress, and go into the everlasting place. Don't turn your face away from me."

The same day, in the Median city of Ecbatana,[1] Sarah the daughter of Raguel was also insulted by her father's woman-slaves because she had been married to seven husbands who Asmodeus[2] the evil spirit[3] had killed before they had lain with her.

"Do you not know," said they, "that you have strangled your husbands? You have already had seven husbands, and you were not named after any of them. Why do you beat us because of them? If they are dead, go be with them, and let us never see either a son or daughter from you."

When she heard these things she was very sad, and she thought of strangling herself, and she said, "I am the only daughter of my father, and if I do this, it will be a reproach against him, and I will bring his old age with sadness to the grave."

Then she prayed towards the window, and said, "Blessed are you, my Lord the god,[4] and your holy and glorious name is blessed and honorable forever. Let all your works praise you forever. Now, Lord, I set I my eyes and my face towards you, say, 'Take me out of the earth, that I may no longer hear the reproach.' You know, Lord, that I am pure from all sin with man, and that I never polluted my name, or the name of my father, in the land of my captivity. I am the only daughter of my father, and he has no child to be his heir, nor any near relative, or any son of his alive to whom I may offer myself to as a wife. My seven husbands are already dead, and why should I live? If it does not please you that I should die, command some thought to be had of me, and pity taken of me, that I hear no more insults."

The prayers of them both were heard before the majesty of the great God, and great (God and send Lord) Raphael (the messenger himself,)[5] was sent to heal them both, to remove the scales from the whiteness of Tobit's eyes, and to give Sarah the daughter of Raguel as a wife to Tobiah the son of Tobit, and to bind Asmodeus the evil spirit, because she belonged to Tobiah by right of inheritance. When Tobit came home and entered his house, Sarah the daughter of Raguel came down from her upper room.

Tobit (Vaticanus): Chapter 3 Notes

1) Codex Vaticanus: Ekbatanois (ЄКВΛΤΛΝΟΙϹ)

- Septuagint ms. 243: Ecbasanoes (Ἐκβασανοις)
- Codex Complutensis 1 (VL 109): Bethanis
- Ge'ez manuscripts: Bathani (ቢጣኒ)

Ecbatana was the capital of the Median Empire, and later the summer capital of the Persian Empire. Its name translates in old Persian as 'the place of gathering.'

2) Codex Vaticanus: Asmodaus (ΛϹΜΟΔΛΥϹ)

- Codex Sinaiticus: Asmodeos (ΛϹΜΟΔЄΟϹ)
- Septuagint ms. 319: Asmodeus (Ἀσμοδευς)
- Septuagint ms. 46: Asmodaeon (Ἀσμοδαιον)
- Codex Bobbiensis (VL 135): Asmadeum
- Codex Complutensis 1 (VL 109): Nasbodeus

Asmodeus is a Jewish and Samaritan demon, adopted from the Zoroastrian faith. The name is derived from the Avestan aēšəma daēuua (اسمودیوس و اسمودئوس), which translates as wrath-demon. At the time, Zoroastrianism was one of the religions practiced in Media.

3) Codex Vaticanus: to ponêron daemonion (ΤΟ ΠΟΝΗΡΟΝ ΔΛΙΜΟΝΙΟΝ). Translation: the wrathful (or painful, oppressive, grievous) demon (or divine, lesser god, powerful spirit)

- Codex Sinaiticus: to daemonion to ponêron (**ΤΟ ΔΑΙΜΟΝΙΟΝ ΤΟ ΠΟΝΗΡΟΝ**). Translation: the demon (or divine, lesser god, powerful spirit) the wrathful (or painful, oppressive, grievous)

The Greek term has many interpretations, and at its core relates to something powerful. As the being in question was a Zoroastrian demon, the original term used in the Aramaic text was likely and Aramaic translation of the Avestan term aēšma daēuua (ܘ ܣ܊ܩ܊ܐ)(ܣܩ) ܣ܊ܩ܊ܣ܊), which translates as 'wrath demon.'

4) Codex Vaticanus: Cyrie o theos (**ΚΥΡΙΕΟΘΕΟC**). Translation: lord the god

- Septuagint ms. 126: Cyrios o theos (**Κυριος ο θεος**). Translation: lord the god

Based on the Aramaic sections of Masoretic Daniel that were not translated into Hebrew, the original Aramaic term the Greeks translated as 'Lord the god' was almost certainly adonai ha'elohim (אֲדֹנָי הָאֱלֹהִים), which in Aramaic means 'lord of the gods,' however, interpreted in Neo-Assyrian or Neo-Babylonian means 'lord the god.'

5) Codex Vaticanus: megalou Raphaêl (**ΜΕΓΑΛΟΥΡΑΦΑΗΛ**). Translation: great Raphael

- Septuagint ms. 126: megalou Theos cae apestile Cyrios Raphaêl ton angelon autou (**μεγαλου Θεος και απεστειλε Κυριος Ραφαηλ τον αγγελον αυτου**). Translation: great god and sent Lord Raphael the messenger himself

- Septuagint ms. 311: megalou apestal Raphaêl (**μεγαλου απεσταλ Ραφαηλ**). Translation: great apostle Raphael

Tobit (Vaticanus): Chapter 3 Notes

Raphael was a messenger in some Judahites sects and later adopted by Christians and Muslims. Raphael only appears in the books of Tobit and the Watchers (1st Enoch). Both seem to have been important to Essen communities later, and neither was of interest to the Pharisees or Sadducees. As Josephus claimed the Essenes considered themselves to be descents of the ancient Canaanites, it is plausible that this name started as a reference to a healing god.

Tobit (Vaticanus): Chapter 4

On that day, Tobit remembered the silver that he had committed to Gabael in the city of Ray in Media, and said to himself, "I have wished for death, therefore, I will call for my son Tobiah that I may sign over to him of the silver before I die."

He called him and he said, "My son when I am dead, bury me, and don't neglect your mother, but honor her all the days of your life, and do that which will please her, and do not grieve her. Remember, my son, that she saw many dangers for you when you were in her womb, and when she is dead, bury her next to me in the same grave."

"My son, be mindful of our Lord the god all your days and don't let your will be set to sin or to transgress his commandments. Do correctly all your life, and don't follow the ways of unrighteousness. If you deal honestly, your business will prosper and you will succeed."

"Give to charities from your property, and when you give charitably, don't let your eye be envious, nor turn your face from any of the poor, and the face of God will not be turned away from you."

"If you have abundance give charitably accordingly, but if you have but a little, do not be afraid to give according to that little. You lay up a good treasure for yourself against the day of necessity. Because that charity delivers from death and allows not to come into darkness. Charity is a good gift to all that give it in the sight of the Highest."

"Beware of all whores my son, and make sure to take a wife from one of your relatives, and don't take a foreign woman as a wife, who is not of your father's tribe. We are the children of the prophets, Noah, Abraham, Isaac, and Jacob. Remember, my son, that our fore-fathers from the beginning, they all married wives of their own families, and were blessed in their children, and their seed will inherit the land."

"Now, therefore, my son, love your brothers and don't despise in your heart your brothers, the sons, and daughters of your people, in not taking a wife of them. In pride comes, destruction and much trouble, and in lewdness is decay and great lack, for lewdness is the mother of famine."

"Don't let the wages of any man, who has worked for you remain with you, but give him it out of hand, for if you serve God, he will also repay you. Be circumspect my son, in all things you do, and be wise in all your conversation. Don't do that which you hate to any man."

"Don't drink wine until you are drunken, nor let drunkenness go with you in your journey. Give of your bread to the hungry, and of your garments to them that are naked, and according to your abundance give charitably.

"Don't let your eye be envious when you give to charity. Pour out your bread on the burial of the just, but give nothing to the wicked. Ask counsel of all that are wise, and don't despise any profitable counsel."

"Bless your Lord the god always, and desire of him that your ways may be directed, and that all your paths and counsels may prosper, for every nation has no counsel, but the Lord himself gives all good things, and he humbles whom he will, as he will."

"Now, therefore, my son, remember my commandments, neither let them be put out of your mind. I signify this to them, that I committed ten talents to Gabael ben Gabri at Ray in Media. Don't be afraid, my son, that we are made poor, for you have much wealth, if you fear God, and leave from all sin, and do that which is pleasing in his sight."

Tobit (Vaticanus): Chapter 5

Tobiah answered him, "Father, I will do all things which you have commanded me. But how can I receive the silver, seeing I do not know him?"

Then he gave him the handwritten message, and said to him, "Find a man who will go with you, while I yet live, and I will pay him wages. Then go and receive the silver."

Therefore, when he went to seek the man, he found Raphael, who was a messenger.[1] He did not know, and he asked him, "Can you go with me to Ray? Do you know the place well?"

The messenger answered, "I will go with you, and I know the road well, as I have lodged with our brother Gabael."

Then Tobiah told him, "Wait for me until I tell my father."

He replied to him, "Go, and don't delay."

He went in and said to his father, "Look, I have found one who will go with me."

Then he stated, "Call him to me, that I may know of what tribe he is, and whether he is a trustworthy man to go with you."

So he called him, and he came in, and they greeted one another. Then Tobit asked him, "Brother, tell me of what tribe and family you are."

He answered, "Are you looking for a tribe or family, or a hired man to go with your son?"

Then Tobit said to him, "I would know, brother, your families, and name."

Then he answered, "I am Azariah, the son of Hananiah the great, and of your brothers."

Then Tobit replied, "You are welcome, brother. Do not be angry with me, because I have inquired to know your tribe and your family, for you are my brother, of an honest and good stock. I know Hananiah and Iathan, sons of that great Shemaiah, as we went together to Jerusalem to worship, and offered the firstborn, and the tenths of the fruits, and they were not seduced with the error of our brothers. My brother, you are of good stock. But tell me, what wages will I give you? Will you take a beka[2] a day, and costs equal to my son's?"

"Yes."

"Also, if you return safe, I will add a bonus to your wages."

So they were very pleased, and he said to Tobiah, "Prepare yourself for the journey, and God send you on a good journey."

When his son had prepared all things for the journey, his father said, "Travel with this man, and Shamayim Baitylos[3] will bring success to your journey, and his messenger will accompany you."

So they left together, along with the young man's dog, but Hannah his mother wept, and asked Tobit, "Why have you sent away our son? Is he not the staff of our hand, going in and out before us? Do not be greedy to add silver to silver, but let it be as garbage in comparison to our child, Amen![4] For that which the Lord has given us to live with is enough for us."

Tobit replied to her, "Don't worry, my sister, he will return in safety, and your eyes will see him. For the good messenger will keep him company, and his journey will be prosperous, and he will return safe," and so she stopped crying.

Tobit (Vaticanus): Chapter 5 Notes

1) Codex Vaticanus: angelos (ᴀⲅⲅⲉⲗⲟⲥ). Translation: messenger

- Codex Sinaiticus: angelos tou theou (ᴀⲅⲅⲉⲗⲟⲥⲧⲟⲩⲑⲉⲟⲩ). Translation: messenger of the god

- Septuagint ms. 236: angelon ($\alpha\gamma\gamma\epsilon\lambda o\nu$). Translation: messenger

- Septuagint ms. 71: angelos Cyriou ($\alpha\gamma\gamma\epsilon\lambda o\varsigma$ Kυριου). Translation: messenger of Lord

2) Codex Vaticanus: drachmên (ⲇⲣⲁⲭⲙⲏⲛ)

- Codex Corbeiensis (VL 150): didragmam

The drachma was a Greek coin used from around 1100 BC, worth approximately 4.3 grams of silver. The name drachma was used in the Septuagint as a translation for the beka (בֶּקַע), was the half-shekel measurement used in ancient Canaan. As 'drachma' was the Greek translation of beka, the term beka is restored.

3) Codex Vaticanus: ouranô oecôn thcos (ⲟⲩⲣⲁⲛⲱⲟⲓⲕⲱⲛ ⲑⲉⲟⲥ). Translation: Uranus (or sky) house god

- Codex Sinaiticus: theos o en tô ouranô (ⲑⲉⲟⲥⲟⲉⲛⲧⲱ ⲟⲩⲣⲁⲛⲱ). Translation: god that is the Uranus (or sky)

The proper name of Uranus is used in this version of the Septuagint, however, could not have been in the Aramaic source text the Greeks used. The name is also found in other versions of Tobit, such as the Codex Sinaiticus' version, and so it is likely that it was in the original Greek translation. The early-Israelite version of Uranus was Shamayim, which may have been in the original Aramaic text, however, the following two words oecôn theos (οἰκῶν θεὸς) were used as a Greek translation for Bethel (ᘝᘜᘙᘘᘗ), which was the name of an earlier Canaanite sky-god, widely worshiped in Samaria, where his major religious center was located: Bethel. Based on the writings of Jeremiah and Baruch, the god Bethel continued to be worshiped in Judah until the kingdom was conquered by the Babylonians.

The Canaanite god Bethel, whose name means 'house of god,' was widely worshiped across Canaan, Anatolia, and the Aegean during the late bronze-age, and was likely a version of the Egyptian goddess Hathor, whose name meant 'House of Ra.' Based on Baruch's description of his god, the god in question was Shemesh, the Canaanite sun-god, which mirrors the role of Ra in the Egyptian pantheon. The alternate name of Bethel in modern literature, Baitylos, is derived from Sanchuniathon's Phoenician History, which was originally published sometime in the late bronze age. Baitylos is used to differentiate the god from the town named after him, however, both were pronounced the same in ancient Canaanite, Aramaic, and Hebrew. Bethel was also the word for 'meteorite,' and shrines dedicated to Baitylos were built as meteorite impact sites across the Mediterranean, and continued to be worshiped in Northwest Africa as late as the 5th-century AD.

As Uranus was a translation, presumably of Shamayim, and 'house god' is clearly a translation of Baitylos, Shamayim Baitylos is used in this translation. These names were also used interchangeably by Jeremiah and Baruch.

Tobit (Vaticanus): Chapter 6

As they traveled on their journey they traveled down the Tigris River, and one evening they camped on the bank. When the young man went down to wash, a fish leaped out of the river and would have eaten him, but the messenger shouted to him, "Catch the fish!"

The young man grabbed hold of the fish and pulled it onto land, and the messenger said, "Cut open the fish, and take the heart and the liver and the guts, and keep them safe."

So the young man did as the messenger commanded him, and when they had roasted the fish, they ate it, then they both went on their way until they arrived at Ecbatana. Then the young man asked the messenger, "Brother Azariah, to what use is the heart and the liver and the guts of the fish?"

He said to him, "Touch the heart and the liver, if a demon or a destructive spirit[1] troubles you in any way. If we smoke them before a man or woman, the party will no longer be cursed. As for the guts, it is good to anoint a man that has whiteness in his eyes, and he will be healed."

When they had come close to Ray, the messenger said to the young man, "Brother, today we will lodge with Raguel, who is your cousin. He has only one daughter, named Sarah. I will ask for her, that she may be given to you as a wife. You have the right to claim her, seeing you are the only one of her family left. The girl is good-looking and wise. Now, hear me and I will speak to her father, and when we return from Ray we will celebrate the marriage. I know that Raguel can't marry her to another according to the law of Moses, as he will be guilty of death, because the right of inheritance applies to you rather than to any other."

Then the young man answered the messenger, "I have heard, brother Azariah that this girl has been given to seven men, who all died in the marriage chamber. Now, I am my father's only son, and I am afraid, in case if I go into her, I will die, like the others before me. A wicked spirit loves her, which hurts anybody who comes to her. Therefore, I also fear in case I die, and bring my father's and my mother's life to the grave with sorrow because of me, for they have no other son to bury them."

Then the messenger said to him, "Don't you remember the commands which your father gave you, that you should marry a wife of your own family? Therefore hear me, my brother, for she will be given to you as a wife, and don't be concerned about the evil spirit, for this very night will she be given you in marriage. When you will enter your bride, take the ashes of incense and will lay on them the heart and liver of the fish, and make a smoke with it. The demon will smell it, and flee, and not return for ages and ages. When you come to her, both of you rise and pray to the gracious god, to save you and have mercy on you. Have no fears, as she is appointed to you from the beginning. You will save her, and she will go with you, and she will carry your children."

Now when Tobiah had heard these things, he loved her, and his heart was effectually joined to her.

Tobit (Vaticanus): Chapter 6 Notes

1) Codex Vaticanus: daemonion ê paneuma ponêron (ⲆⲀⲒⲘⲞⲚⲒⲞⲚ Ⲏ ⲦⲦⲀⲚⲈⲨⲘⲀ ⲦⲞⲚⲎⲢⲞⲚ). Translation: demon (or lesser god, powerful spirit, divinity) or (or as) spirit (or wind, breath, life, air, angel) destructive (or painful, grievous)

• Codex Sinaiticus: daemoniou ê pneumatos ponêrou (ⲆⲀⲒⲘⲞⲚⲒⲞⲨ Ⲏ ⲦⲦⲚⲈⲨⲘⲀⲦⲞⲤ ⲦⲞⲚⲎⲢⲞⲨ). Translation: demon (or lesser god, powerful spirit, divinity) or (or as) spirit (or wind, breath, life, air, angel) destructive (or painful, grievous)

• Septuagint manuscript 71: daemonion (δαιμονιον). Translation: demon (or lesser god, powerful spirit, divinity)

The phrase appears to originate in the Zoroastrian terms daeva (دَيُوَه_ج), meaning 'demon,' and Angra Mainyu (اَنگرَمَئِینُیُو), meaning 'destructive spirit.'

54

Tobit (Vaticanus): Chapter 7

When they arrived in Ecbatana, and reached the house of Raguel, Sarah met them, and after they had greeted one another, she brought them into the house. Then Raguel asked Edna his wife, "How much does this young man look like my cousin Tobit!"

Raguel asked them, "From where are you, brothers?"

They replied, "We are of the Naphtalites, which are captives in Nineveh."

Then he asked them, "Do you know Tobit our relative?"

They answered, "We know him."

Then he asked, "Is he in good health?"

They answered, "He is both alive, and in good health," and Tobiah added, "he is my father."

Then Raguel leaped up, and kissed him, and wept, blessed him, and said to him, "You are the son of an honest and good man!" But when he had heard that Tobit was blind, he was sad and wept, and Edna his wife, and also Sarah his daughter wept.

Nevertheless, they entertained them cheerfully, and after that, they killed a ram from the flock, and they set the meat on the table. Then Tobiah said to Raphael,

"Brother Azariah, speak of those things of which you talked along the road, and let this business be finished."

So he communicated the matter with Raguel, and Raguel said to Tobiah, "Eat and drink, and celebrate, for it is decided that you should marry my daughter! However, I will tell you the truth. I have given my daughter in marriage to seven men, who died the night they came into her. Nevertheless, for now, celebrate."

Tobiah replied, "I will eat nothing here, until we agree and swear one to another."

Raguel said, "Then take her from now on according to our custom, as you are her cousin, and she is yours, and the merciful God gave you good success in all things."

Then he called his daughter Sarah, and she came to her father, and he took her by the hand, and gave her to Tobiah as a wife, saying, "Look, take her according to the laws of Moses, and take her away to your father."

He blessed them, and called Edna his wife, and took a book and wrote a contract and sealed it. Then they began to eat. Afterward, Raguel called his wife Edna, and said to her, "Sister, prepare another room, and take her in there."

When she had done as he had ordered her, she brought her there, and she wept, and she received the tears of her daughter, and said to her, "Have courage, my child. The Lord of the sky and the earth give family to replace your sorrow, so be courageous my daughter."

Tobit (Vaticanus): Chapter 8

When they had eaten, they took Tobiah to her. As he went, he remembered the words of Raphael, and took the ashes of the incense, and put the heart and the liver of the fish on them, and smoked it. When the evil spirit smelled the odor, he fled for the farthest parts of Egypt, but the messenger caught him. When they were both behind closed doors, Tobiah rose out of the bed, and said, "Sister, rise, and let us pray that the Lord will have pity on us."

Then Tobiah prayed, "Blessed are you, god of our fathers, and blessed is your holy and glorious name forever. Let the skies bless you, and all your creatures. You made Adam and gave him Eve his wife as a helper, and from them came mankind. You said, 'It is not good that man should be alone, let us make for him a helper like himself.' Now, Lord, I do not take my sister like a prostitute, but uprightly, therefore mercifully ordain that we may become old together."

She said with him, "Amen."

So they slept together that night. Raguel arose, and went and dug a grave, saying, "I'm afraid that he is also dead." And when Raguel returned to his house, he told his wife Edna, "Send one of the girls, and let her see whether he is alive, if he is not, we can bury him before anyone finds out."

So the girl opened the door, and went in, and found them both asleep, and she returned and told them that he was alive. Then Raguel praised god, and said, "God, you are worthy to be praised with all pure and holy praise, therefore let your holy ones praise you with all your creatures, and let all your messengers and your elect praise you forever. You are to be praised, for you have made me joyful. It has not happened, that which I suspected, but you have dealt with us according to your great mercy. You are to be praised because you have had mercy on two that were the only begotten children of their fathers. Grant them mercy, Lord, and finish their life in health with joy and mercy."

Then Raguel commanded his servants to refill the grave. He kept the wedding feast fourteen days. For before the days of the marriage were finished, Raguel had said to him by an oath, that he should not leave until the fourteen days of the marriage were expired. Then he should take half of his goods, and go in safety to his father, and should have the rest, "when I and my wife are dead."

Tobit (Vaticanus): Chapter 9

Then Tobiah called Raphael, and said to him, "Brother Azariah, take with you a servant, and two camels, and go to Ray in Media to Gabael, and bring me the silver, and bring him to the wedding. Raguel has sworn that I will not leave, yet my father counts the days, and if I am too long, he will be very concerned. So Raphael went out, and lodged with Gabael, and gave him the handwritten message, and he brought out bags which were sealed up and gave them to him. Early in the morning they went out both together and came to the wedding, and Tobiah blessed his wife.

Tobit (Vaticanus): Chapter 10

His father Tobit counted every day and when the days of the journey were up and they had not returned, then Tobit asked, "Are they delayed, or is Gabael dead, and there is no man to give him the silver?"

Therefore he was very sad, and his wife said to him, "My son is dead," as he had stayed away so long. She began to wail and said to him, "Now I care for nothing! My son! Since I have let you go, the light of my eyes!"

To which Tobit replied, "Be silent! Don't be worried as he is safe."

But she replied, "You be silent, and stop lying to me! My son is dead!"

She went out every day to the road they had left on, and ate no food throughout the day, and did not stop mourning her son Tobiah all night until the fourteen days of the wedding had expired, which Raguel had sworn that he should spend there. Then Tobiah said to Raguel, "Let me go, as my father and mother will be looking for me."

But his father-in-law said to him, "Remain with me, and I will send a message to your father, and they will tell him how you are doing."

But Tobiah answered, "No, let me go to my father."

Then Raguel rose and gave him Sarah, his wife, and half his property, slaves, livestock, and silver. He blessed them, and sent them away, saying, "The god of the sky gives you a prosperous journey, my children," and he said to his daughter, "Honor your father and your mother in law, which are now your parents, so I may hear good things of you," and he kissed her.

Edna said to Tobiah, "The Lord of the skies[1] return you, my dear brother, and grant that I may see your children through my daughter Sarah before I die, that I may rejoice before the Lord. Look, I am trusting my daughter to you, do not mistreat her."

After this, Tobiah went his way, praising God that he had given him a prosperous journey, and blessed Raguel and Edna his wife.

Tobit (Vaticanus): Chapter 10 Notes

1) Codex Vaticanus: o theos tou ouranou (OΘЄOCTOY OYPANOY). Translation: the god the vaulted-sky

• Codex Sinaiticus: o cyrios tou ourano (OKYPIOCTOY OYPANO). Translation: the lord the vaulted-sky

• Codex Alexandrinus: o cyrios tou ourano (O ΘЄOC TOY OYPANO TЄKNA). Translation: the god of the vaulted-sky's child (or descendant)

• Septuagint manuscript 107: ho cyrios Theos tou ouranou (ὁ κύριος Θεος τοῦ οὐρανοῦ). Translation: the lord God of the sky

The vaulted-sky (Οὐρανοῦ) of early Greek cosmology was based on, or very similar to, the Shamayim of the ancient Canaanite and Israelite religions. The Shamayim was the first thing created in Genesis, right before Eretz (Earth).

Tobit (Vaticanus): Chapter 11

He traveled the roads until they arrived at Nineveh, and then Raphael said to Tobiah, "You know, brother, how you left your father. Let's hurry ahead of your wife, and prepare the house. Take the guts of the fish in your hand." So they went their way, along with the dog.

Hannah was sitting looking down the road for her son, and when she saw him coming, she said to his father, "Look, your son comes, along with the man that went with him!"

Then Raphael said, "I know, Tobiah, that your father will open his eyes. So anoint his eyes with the guts, and they will become itchy and he will rub them, and the whiteness will fall away, and he will see you."

Then Hannah ran out, and fell on the neck of her son, and said to him, "Now that I have seen you, my son, I am content to die from now on!"

They both wept. Tobit also went out towards the door and stumbled, but his son ran to him and took hold of his father, and he rubbed the guts on his fathers' eyes, saying, "Be hopeful my father."

When his eyes began to itch, he rubbed them, and the whiteness fell away from the corners of his eyes, and when he saw his son, he fell on his neck. He wept and said, "Blessed are you, God, and blessed is your name forever! Blessed are all your holy messengers! For you have scourged, and have taken pity on me! Look, I see my son Tobiah!"

His son went in celebrating, and told his father the great things that had happened to him in Media. Then Tobit went out to meet his daughter-in-law at the gate of Nineveh, rejoicing and praising God, and those who saw him go by marveled because his sight had been restored. But Tobiah gave thanks before them that God had mercy on him. When he approached Sarah his daughter-in-law, he blessed her saying, "You are welcome, daughter. Blessed is the God who has brought you to us, and blessed is your father and your mother."

There was joy among all his brothers who were in Nineveh. Ahikar and his nephew Nadan[1] came, and Tobiah's wedding was celebrated seven days with great joy.

Tobit (Vaticanus): Chapter 10 Notes

1) Codex Vaticanus: Nasbas (ⲚⲀⳞⲂⲀⳞ)

• Codex Sinaiticus: Nabad (ⲚⲀⲂⲀⲆ)

• Septuagint manuscript 71: Nabas (Ναβασ)

• Sahidic manuscripts: Asbas (ⲀⳞⲂⲀⳞ)

• Codex Complutensis 1 (VL 190): Nabat

• Codex Regius (VL 148): Nabal

• Codex Monacensis (VL 130): Nadab

The name of the nephew is not standardized in the manuscripts. The nephew's name used in the surviving copies of the Words of Ahikar is Nadan, which is used in this translation as the copies of the Septuagint do not agree.

Tobit (Vaticanus): Chapter 12

Then Tobit called his son Tobiah and said to him, "My son, see that the man who went with you is paid, and you must give him a bonus."

Tobiah said to him, "Father, it won't hurt me to give him half of everything which I have brought, as he has brought me back to you in safety, and saved my wife, and brought the silver to me, and also healed you."

Then the old man said, "It is due to him," so he called the messenger, and he said to him, "Take half of all that you have brought, and leave in safety."

Then he took them both separately, and said to them, "Bless God, praise him, and exalt him, and thank him for the things which he has done to you in the sight of all that live. It is good to praise God, and exalt his name, and honorably to declare the works of God, and so don't be slow to praise him. It is good to keep private the secret of a king, but it is honorable to reveal the works of God. Do that which is good, and no evil will touch you. Prayer is good with fasting and charity and righteousness. A little with righteousness is better than much with unrighteousness."

"It is better to give charitably than to save up gold, for charity delivers from death, and will purge away all sin. Those who exercise charity and righteousness will be filled with life, but they who sin are enemies to their own life. Certainly, I will take nothing from you. For I said, 'It was good to keep private the secret of a king, but that it was honorable to reveal the works of God.'"

"Now, therefore, when you prayed, and Sarah your daughter-in-law, I brought your prayers before Qetesh,[1] and when you buried the dead, I was also with you. When you did not delay to rise and leave your dinner to go bury the dead, your good deed was not hidden from me, but I was with you. And so, God has sent me to heal you, and Sarah your daughter-in-law. I am Raphael, one of the seven holy messengers, which present the prayers of the saints, and which go in and out before the glory of Qetesh."

Then they were both troubled, and fell on their faces, for they were afraid. But he said to them, "Don't be afraid, for it will be well with you. Praise God, and do not ask any favor from me. By the will of our God I came, therefore praise him forever. All these days I appeared to you, but I did not eat or drink, as you were seeing a vision. Now, therefore, give God thanks, for I go up to him that sent me. Write all the things which were done in a book."

When they rose, they no longer saw him. Then they confessed the great and wonderful works of God, and how the messenger of the Lord had appeared to them.

Tobit (Vaticanus): Chapter 12 Notes

1) Codex Vaticanus: agiou (ᴀᴦıᴏʏ). Translation: saint

• Codex Sinaiticus: doxês cyriou (ᴅᴏᴤʜᴄᴋʏᴘıᴏʏ). Translation: glorious (or magnificent, splendorous) lord

• Septuagint ms. 542: Theo (Θεο). Translation: God

The term hagiou (Ἁγίου) is used in the Septuagint, where the Masoretic texts retain the word Qetesh (קדש), which was the title of the Israelite goddess Asherah, whose worship would later be banned by the Judahite king Josiah.

Tobit (Vaticanus): Chapter 13

Tobit wrote a prayer of joy and said,

> "Blessed is God that lives for ages, and blessed in his kingdom. For he punishes and has mercy. He leads down to the grave and brings up again. Neither are there any that can avoid his hand. Tell of him to the nations you Israelites, for he has scattered us among them. Declare his greatness and extol him before all the living, for he is our Lord, and he is the god of our father for ages. He will scourge us for our iniquities, and have mercy again, and will gather us out of all nations, among whom he has scattered us."

> "If you turn to him with your whole heart, and with your whole mind, and deal honestly before him, then will he return to you, and will not hide his face from you. Praise Lord Sydyk,¹ and praise the king of ages. In the land of my captivity, I praise him and declare his might and majesty to a sinful nation. You returned sinners, sang of justice before him. Who knows if he will accept you, and have mercy on you?"

> "I will extol my god, and my mind will praise the king of the sky,² and will rejoice in his greatness. Let all men speak, and let all praise him in Jerusalem. Jerusalem, the holy city, he will scourge you for your children's works and have mercy again on the sons of the righteous. Give praise to the Lord, for he is good, and praise the king of ages, that his tabernacle may

be built in you again with joy, and let him make joyful there in you those that are captives, and love in you forever those that are miserable. Many nations will come from far to the name of Lord the god with gifts in their hands, gifts to the king of the sky, all generations will praise you with great joy. Cursed are all they who hate you, and blessed will all be which love you forever."

"Rejoice and be glad for the children of the just, for they will be gathered together, and will bless the Lord of the just. Blessed are they which love you, for they will rejoice in your peace, blessed are they which have been sorrowful for all your scourges, for they will rejoice for you, when they have seen all your glory, and will be glad forever. Let my mind bless the great god king.³ For Jerusalem will be built up with sapphires and emeralds, and precious stone, your walls and towers and battlements with pure gold. The streets of Jerusalem will be paved with beryl and carbuncle and stones of Sauvira.⁴ All her streets will say, 'Hallelujah,' and they will praise him, saying, 'Blessed is the god who has exalted you forever.'"

Tobit (Vaticanus): Chapter 13 Notes

1) Codex Vaticanus: ton cyrion tês dicaeosynês (ΤΟΝ ΚΥΡΙΟΝ ΤΗCΔΙΚΑΙΟCΥΝΗC). Translation: the lord the justice

- Septuagint manuscript 249: ton theon tês dicaeosynês (τον θεον της δικαιοσυνης). Translation: the god the justice

- Codex Corbeiensis (VL 150): de dominus in iustitia. Translation: the lord in (or under, towards) Justinia

- Codex Bobbiensis (VL 135): de deum de iustitiam. Translation: the god the justice

The term 'the justice' (τῆσ Δικαιοσύνης) was used in the Septuagint for places where the Masoretic Texts retains the name Sydyk (צֶדֶק), the Canaanite god of justice. During the Roman era, the same name was applied to the Roman god Jupiter (Iove) as well as for the Roman spirit of Justice (Iustitia) by Hebrew-speaking people, meaning the knowledge of Sydyk had not disappeared by the early Christian era.

2) Codex Vaticanus: basili tou ouranou (ΒΑCΙΛΕΙΤΟΥΟΥΡΑΝΟΥ). Translation: king the vaulted-sky (or Uranus)

- Codex Complutensis 1 (VL109): regem de caelum. Translation: king of the sky

- Codex Bobbiensis (VL 135): rex de caelum et terrae. Translation: king of the sky and land

The vaulted-sky (Οὐρανοῦ) of early Greek cosmology was based on, or very similar to, the Shamayim of the ancient Canaanite and Israelite religions, however, the term 'king' is more problematic, as the Aramaic word mlch (ΝＹＬＸ) is likely the source of the

Septuagint's word Moloch, the name of one of the gods that Solomon set up an idol to in his temple.

The god in question was the Ammanite god mlk (𐤌𐤋𐤊), whose name translates as king, however, the god's name is not pronounced in Hebrew as melech (מֶלֶךְ), meaning king, but preserves the Aramaic spelling as mwlch (מוֹלִךְ). This verse implies that Moloch was a title for Shamayim and Bethel, who certainly was a god being worshiped in the Temple in Jerusalem before King Josiah's reforms circa 625 BC, several decades after this book was apparently written.

3) Codex Vaticanus: ton theon ton basilea ton megan (ΤΟΝ ΘΕΟΝΤΟΝΒΑϹΙΛΕΑΤΟΝΜΕΓΑΝ). Translation: the god the king the great

• Codex Sinaiticus: ton cyrion ton basilea ton megan (ΤΟΝ ΚΥΡΙΟΝ ΤΟΝ ΒΑϹΙΛΕΑ ΤΟΝ ΜΕΓΑΝ). Translation: the god the king the great

• Septuagint manuscript 58: ton theon ton basilea ton mega (τον Θεον τον βασιλεα τον μεγα). Translation: the god the king the great

Given the pronunciation of 'king' in Aramaic, this may have read 'the god Moloch the great,' however, that cannot be proven with the surviving texts, and so a more generalized translation is used.

4) Codex Vaticanus: Souphir (ϹΟΥΦΙΡ)

• Codex Sinaiticus: Souphir (ϹΟΥΦΕΙΡ)

• Septuagint manuscript 46: Ophir (Οφειρ)

• Septuagint manuscript 583: Saphir (Σαφιρ)

• Septuagint manuscript 319: Souphêrô (Σουφηρω)

• Septuagint manuscript 107: Souphêrô (Σουφηρ)

This quasi-mythical land of riches was also transliterated as Sophira (Σωφηρα) in other books of the Septuagint, and as Ofir (אוֹפִיר) in the Masoretic Texts.

The location of this civilization has been a matter of debate for ages. Given the list of items imported from Souphir/Sophira/Ofir, it was likely the ancient Pakistani Kingdom of Sauvira on the Indus River. Imported items include gold, silver, sandalwood, pearls, ivory, apes, and peacocks. Sandalwood trees are indigenous to South and Southeast Asia and have traditionally been considered sacred by the Hindus, Jainists, Buddhists, and Zoroastrians, as well as other Asian cultures. Peacocks are indigenous to South and Southeast Asia, as well as the Congo Rain-forest, however, Sandalwood trees are not found in the Congo Rain-forest. Apes were still living in South and Southeast Asia circa 1000 BC, along with most of Africa. An alternate theory regarding the location of Sophira was that it was a trading port in Southern Arabia or Somalia, however, the ships of Solomon were said to take three years to travel between Edom and Souphir/Sophira/Ofir, which makes the location of Sauvira more likely.

The Kingdom of Sauvira is listed in the ancient Late Vedic period and early Buddhist literature, as well as the Mahabharata, based around its capital of Rohri in the modern Pakistani state of Sindh.

This civilization is recorded as having existed from the Early Vedic period, before 1100 BC, meaning it would have existed in the time of Solomon. The capital of Sauvira was Aror, also called Roruka or Rorik in classical literature, which was one of the most important cities in South Asia in the 7th-century BC, when this book was set. According to the Buddhist Bhallatiya Jataka, as well as Jain Story of Udayan and the town of Vitabhaya, the city of Aror was destroyed by a major sandstorm around 450 BC, following which the modern city of Rorhi (روهـڙي / روبـڙى) was founded around 10 kilometers away.

Tobit (Vaticanus): Chapter 14

Tobit finished praising God.

He was 58 years old when he lost his sight, which was restored to him after 8 years.[1] He gave charitably, and he increased in his respect for Lord the god and praised him. When he was very old he called his son, and the sons of his son, and said to him, "My son, take your children, for look, I am old, and am ready to leave this life. Go into Media my son, for I certainly believe those things which Jonah the prophet said of Nineveh, that it will be overthrown.[2]

That for a time peace will be in Media, and that our brothers will lie scattered in the earth from that good land, and Jerusalem will be desolate, and the Temple of God in it will be burnt and will be desolate for a time, so again God will have mercy on them, and bring them back into the land, where they will build a temple, but not like the first, until the time of that age is finished, and afterward, they will return from all places of their captivity, and build up Jerusalem gloriously, and the Temple of God will be built in it forever with a glorious building, as the prophets have spoken of.

All nations will turn, and fear Lord the god truly, and will bury their idols, and the nations will praise the Lord, and his people will confess God, and the Lord will exalt his people, and all those which love Lord the god in truth and justice will rejoice, showing mercy to our brothers.

Now, my son, leave Nineveh because those things which the prophet Jonah spoke will certainly happen. But follow the law and the commandments, and show yourself merciful and just, that it may go well with you. Bury me decently, and your mother with me, but remain no longer in Nineveh."

"Child, remember what they did to Nadan.[3] Ahikar,[4] nursed him, yet he brought him out of the light into darkness, and what he returned to him, and Ahikar did not save him, but to him the repayment was given, and he went down into darkness. Manasseh[5] gave charitably, and escaped the snares of death which they had set for him, but Nadan[6] fell into the snare and perished. Therefore now, my son, consider what charity does, and how righteousness does deliver."

When he had said these things, he died in the bed at 158 years old, and he buried him honorably. When Hannah his mother was dead, he buried her with his father. Then Tobiah departed with his wife and children to Ecbatana to Raguel his father-in-law, where he became old with honor, and he buried his father and mother in law honorably, and he inherited their property, and his father Tobit's. He died at Ecbatana in Media, being 127 years old. But before he died he heard of the destruction of Nineveh, which was taken by Nebuchadnezzar and Xerxes,[7] and before his death, he rejoiced over Nineveh.

Tobit (Vaticanus): Chapter 14 Notes

1) Based on the chronology within the story, as Tobit lost his sight in 681 BC, and therefore this was the year 673 BC.

2) Codex Vaticanus: Iônas (ιωΝΑC)

- Codex Sinaiticus: Naoum (ΝΑΟΥΜ)

Both Nahum and Jonah predicted the destruction of Nineveh. The Book of Nahum is internally dated sometime during and shortly after the Assyrian occupation of Egypt between 663 and 656 BC, and generally accepted as dating to that era, while Jonah is widely regarded as being fiction by historians.

The Book of Jonah is internally dated sometime during the Assyrian rule of Samaria, approximately 720 to 612 BC. If Jonah and Tobit were both real people, they would have been in Nineveh at the same time, and given the size of the Samaritan population in Nineveh, likely would have met.

3) Codex Vaticanus: Adam (ΑΔΑΜ)

- Codex Sinaiticus: Nadab (ΝΑΔΑΒ)
- Septuagint manuscript 535: Adad (Αδαδ)
- Septuagint manuscript 670: Naman (Ναμαν)
- Sahidic manuscripts: Adar (ⲇⲁⲁⲣ)
- Codex Monacensis (VL 130): Nabad
- Codex Complutensis 1 (VL 109): Nabat
- Codex Bobbiensis (VL 135): Nabath

TOBIT (VATICANUS): CHAPTER 14 NOTES

4) Codex Vaticanus: Achiacharô (ⲁⲭⲓⲁⲭⲁⲣⲱ)

- Codex Sinaiticus: Achicarô (ⲁⲭⲉⲓⲕⲁⲣⲱ)

- Septuagint ms. 670: Achiacharou (Ⲁⲭⲓⲁⲭⲁⲣⲟⲩ)

- Septuagint ms. 319: Agiacharô (Ⲁⲅⲓⲁⲭⲁⲣⲱ)

- Sahidic manuscripts: Akhiaros (ⲁ̄ⲭⲓⲁⲣⲟⲥ)

- Codex Complutensis 1 (VL 109): Acicarum

- Codex Bobbiensis (VL 135): Achicharo

5) Codex Vaticanus: Manassês (ⲘⲀⲚⲀⲤⲤⲎⲤ)

- Codex Sinaiticus: Nadab (Ⲛⲁⲇⲁⲃ)

- Codex Monacensis (VL 130): Nabad

- Codex Complutensis 1 (VL 109): Nabat

- Codex Bobbiensis (VL 135): Nabath

King Manasseh, who ruled Judah roughly between 687 and 643 BC, was mentioned in the records of the Assyrian kings Sennacherib, Esarhaddon, and Ashurbanipal, all of which consider Judah a vassal state. According to 2nd Paralipmenon (Masoretic Dibrê Hayyāmîm), King Manasseh was at one point taken to Assyria in chains for some offense, and later restored to throne of Judah. This is believed to have happened during Esarhaddon's rule, between 681 and 669 BC.

It is unclear why Manasseh was mentioned in this verse in most versions of the Septuagint, however, he is not in the corresponding verse in the Sinaiticus version of Tobit, which claims Ahikar gave to charity, not Manasseh. Manasseh may have been a later insertion into the text, like Nebuchadnezzar and Ahasuerus, who are mentioned later in the chapter, in the Vaticanus version, but not the Sinaiticus version, which maintains the correct name of King Cyaxarês.

6) Codex Vaticanus: Adam (ᴀᴅᴀᴍ)

* Codex Sinaiticus: Nadab (ɴᴀᴅᴀʙ)

* Septuagint manuscript 535: Adad (Aδaδ)

* Sahidic manuscripts: Adas (ⲁⲇⲁⲥ)

7) Codex Vaticanus: Nabouchodonosor cae Asyêros (ɴᴀʙᴏʏxᴏᴅᴏɴᴏcᴏp ᴋᴀɪ ᴀcʏʜpᴏc). Translation: Nabouchodonosor and Asyeros

* Codex Sinaiticus: Achiacharos (ᴀxeɪᴀxᴀpᴏc)

* Codex Alexandrinus: Nabouchodonosor cae Asouchros (ɴᴀʙᴏʏxᴏᴅᴏɴᴏcᴏp ᴋᴀɪ ᴀcᴏʏxpᴏc). Translation: Nabouchodonosor and Asouchros

* Septuagint ms. 319: Nabouchodonosor cae Assyêros (Nαβουχοδονοσορ και Aσσυηρος). Translation: Nabouchodonosor and Assyeros

* Septuagint ms. 46: Nabouchodonosor cae Asoêros (Nαβουχοδονοσορ και Aσοηρος). Translation: Nabouchodonosor and Asoeros

* Septuagint ms. 488: Nabouchodonosor cae Assoucros (Nαβουχοδονοσορ και Aσσουκρος). Translation: Nabouchodonosor and Assoucros

This final line appears to be part of an anachronistic redaction. The Babylonian King Nabopolassar sacked Nineveh in 612 BC, along with Median and Persian allies. His son Nebuchadnezzar, who assumed the throne in 605 BC, finally conquered the remnants of the Assyrian forces in Syria at the Battle of Carchemish that same year, however, he did not destroy Nineveh. The name Asyêros (Ασυηρος) is generally accepted as a variant spelling of Ahasuerus (Ασουηρος), the Aramaic name of Xerxes, the Persian king who ruled between 486 and 465 BC.

The Codex Sinaiticus' does not mention either king, but gives credit to King Achiacharos (Αχιαχαρος) of Media, which is likely an attempt to transliterate the name Uvaxštra (𒁹𒌋𒈦𒁕𒊏), which was also transliterated as Cyaxarês (Κυαξάρης) in Greek, from which his common English name is derived. Other ancient versions of his name include the Elamite Makiišturri (𒀭𒈨𒆠𒅖𒌇𒊑), Neo-Babylonian Úaksatar (𒌑𒀝𒊓𒋻), and the Phrygian Ksuwaksaros (ΚϞΟϠΑΥϞΡΟϞ). Cyaxares was the Median king who fought alongside the Babylonian King Nabopolassar at the sack of Nineveh, following which Nineveh became part of his Median Empire. This seems clear proof that the Codex Sinaiticus version of Tobit is older, and more accurate.

Tobit (Sinaiticus): Chapter 1

The book of the words of Tobit,[1] the son of Tobiel, the son of Ananiel, the son of Aduel, the son of Gabael, the son of Raphael, the son of Raguel, of the descendants of Asahel, of the tribe of Naphtali, who in the time of King Sargon II[2] of the Assyrians was led captive out of Tishbe,[3] which is to the right of Kadesh of Naphtali in Galilee near Asher, back along the roadway to the westward sun, on the left of Peor.[4]

I, Tobit, have followed all the days of my life in the ways of truth and justice, and I was very charitable to my brothers from my nation, who came with me as captives to Nineveh in the land of the Assyrians. When I was still young in my own country of Israel, all of my father's tribe of Naphtali abandoned the house of David of my father, and Jerusalem,[5] which was chosen out of all the tribes of Israel that all the tribes should sacrifice there, where the temple and tabernacle[6] of God[7] was consecrated and built for all ages.[8]

All of my brothers and the house of Naphtali, my father, sacrificed to the young calf created by Jeroboam the king of Israel in Dan and on every mountain in Galilee.[9]

I regularly went by myself to Jerusalem at the feasts, as it was ordained to all Israel by an eternal decree, that the first-born, and the first-fruits, and tithe of the animals. The first-born of the sheep I drove to Jerusalem and gave to the priests, the sons of Aaron, for the altar. The tithe of grain, wine, oil, pomegranates, figs, and the rest of the best fruits, I gave to the Levites who served in Jerusalem. A second tenth I would spend on everything in Jerusalem, each year. What was left I gave to the orphans and the widows, and to the proselytes[10] living among the Israelites I contributed to them a third each year, and I ate everything following the ordinances, the commandments about this in the law of Moses, and following the orders of Debora the mother of Ananiel, my father, as I was orphaned when my father was crushed and died.

When I had come to the age of a man, I took a wife from the descendants of our race, and fathered a son through her, and called his name Tobiah. When we were taken prisoners by the Assyrians, and forced to be captives in Nineveh, all of my brothers and those of my tribes, ate the food of the nations, but I didn't. I kept my mind, and did not eat the food of the nations, as I remembered my god in my mind.

The Highest gave me grace and favor before Sargon II, so that I became the purchaser of his provisions, and I was sent to Media[11] frequently in the years before he died. Once, I gave Gabael the brother of Garbi, in the land of Media a bag containing ten talents of silver.

When Sargon II was dead, Sennacherib[12] his son reigned in his place, and the roads to Media were closed and there was no longer any way to travel to Media. In the days of Sargon, I was very charitable to my brothers of my tribes, and gave my bread to the hungry, my clothes to the naked, and if I saw any of my nation dead, or thrown out of the walls of Nineveh, I buried him.

If Sennacherib killed any, when he came back from Judea, in the days of the judgment he made for the king of the sky,[13] against blasphemers and those that spoke profanely of sacred things, I buried them. He killed many of the Israelites in his anger, and their bodies were buried honorably, and looked for by Sennacherib, but not found.

When one of the Ninevites went and told the king about me, that I buried them, I hid, knowing that I was being searched for, as the king wanted me executed, and I fled in fear. Then all my property was seized and there was nothing left to me. All the nobles abandoned me, other than my wife Hannah and my son Tobiah.

Less than forty days passed, before two of his sons killed him,[14] and they fled into the mountains of Urartu,[15] and Esarhaddon[16] his son reigned in his place, who had with him Ahikar[17] my brother Anael's son, who had under his reckoning the entire kingdom, and held the office over the administrators. Ahikar asked about me, and I returned to Nineveh. Ahikar was chief cupbearer, and keeper of the signet, and commander, and accountant, for King Sennacherib of Assyria, and became second to Esarhaddon, and he was my cousin, and from my family.

Tobit (Sinaiticus): Chapter 1 Notes

1) Codex Sinaiticus: Tobith (ⲧⲱⲃⲓⲑ)

- Codex Vaticanus: Tôbit (ⲧⲱⲃⲉⲓⲧ)
- Septuagint manuscript 106: Tôbit (Ⲧⲱβιⲧ)
- Septuagint manuscript 248: Tôbêt (Ⲧⲱβηⲧ)
- Septuagint manuscript 392: Tôbid (Ⲧⲱβειδ)

The names in the various manuscripts of the book of Tobit/Tobith/Tobid are not standardized, including the names of the book itself. This indicates three or more separate translations into Greek, as no one would have a reason to change the names if redacting one to make the other. The more common English name 'Tobit' is used in this translation.

2) Codex Sinaiticus: Enemessarou (ⲉⲛⲉⲙⲉⲥⲥⲁⲣⲟⲩ)

- Septuagint ms. 46: Ennemesarou (Ἐⲛⲛⲉⲙⲉⲥⲁⲣⲟⲩ)
- Septuagint ms. 71: Enemesarou (Ἐⲛⲉⲙⲉⲥⲁⲣⲟⲩ)
- Septuagint ms. 318: Enaimesarou (Ἐⲛⲁιⲙⲉⲥⲁⲣⲟⲩ)
- Septuagint ms. 122: Enemesarrou (Ἐⲛⲉⲙⲉⲥⲁⲣⲣⲟⲩ)
- Septuagint ms. 249: Enemassarou (Ἐⲛⲉⲙⲁⲥⲥⲁⲣⲟⲩ)
- Septuagint ms. 107: Nemessarou (Ⲛⲉⲙⲉⲥⲥⲁⲣⲟⲩ)
- Sahidic manuscripts: Namessaros (Ⲛⲁⲙⲉⲥⲥⲁⲣⲟⲥ)

Based on the rest of the book this must be a reference to Sargon II, King of Assyria between 722 and 705 BC. The name is often mistranslated as Shalmaneser, however, Enemessarou's son is later identified as Sennacherib, who was Sargon II's son. Shalmaneser was recorded in the books of the Kingdoms (Masoretic Kings), as having conquered Samaria, however, while Shalmaneser V's armies did besiege Samaria for three years, he died before Samaria surrendered, and when they surrendered, it was to Sargon II, Shalmaneser V's heir, who recorded in his records that he deported 27,920 Samaritans to Assyria.

This appears to have been an Aramaic translation of his Assyrian name Šarru-kīnum (𒀭𒈗𒁺), with the Assyrian terms inverted to Kīnum-šarru. His name is believed to translate as approximately as 'king who is legitimate,' suggesting the Aramaic translator interpreted then name as 'legitimate king,' and was not basing the reference on a historic record of the king, after his throne name had become standardized, but lived in the era of Sargon II.

Assuming this is a reference to Sargon, which it appears to be, it is notable that in the Book of Isaiah, the name Šarru-kīnum is rendered as Sargôn (סַרְגוֹן), meaning that the Book of Tobit is not dependent on Isaiah, and was likely translated into Aramaic by someone who had not read Isaiah. This supports the author's claims to be a Samaritan living in Assyria, and the dating of the text to the era of the Assyrian Empire. The Hebrew-derived name 'Sargon' is used in this translation, as it is more common in modern English.

3) Codex Sinaiticus: Tishbes (ΘΙϹΒΗϹ)

• Codex Alexandrinus: Thêbês (ΘΗΒΗϹ)

• Peshitta: Tḥbhš (ܬܚܒܫ). Translation: Thebes

• Codex Corbeiensis (VL 150): Bibel

• Codex Sangermanensis 4 (VL 7): Viel

• Codex Complutensis 1 (VL 109): Biel

• Codex Monacensis (VL 130): Cibiel

TOBIT (SINAITICUS): CHAPTER 1 NOTES

- Codex Bobbiensis (VL 135): Sibiel

- Ge'ez ms.: Thêbêsə (ቴቤስ). Translation: Thebes

The Vaticanus and Sinaiticus manuscripts agree that is was the accepted Greek translation of the town called Tishbe (תִּשְׁבֶּ) in Hebrew, however, not all biblical scholars agree that there was a town called Tishbe in the Masoretic Texts. The issue revolves around the meaning of the word tishbi (תִּשְׁבִּי), which could simply be interpreted as 'resident,' however, was traditionally interpreted as Tishbite, meaning someone from Tishbe. The prophet Elijah was recorded as being a Tishbite, or maybe a 'resident,' in the Masoretic Kings (3rd Kingdoms) chapter 17.

The Septuagint's translation is clearer, where he is recorded as being a Tishbite from Tishbe (Θεσβίτης ἐκ Θεσβων), and so this translation accepts the traditional interpretation of the name Tishbe. It is significant though, that Elijah was closely connected with the Assyrian Samaritans on the Khabur River, where he saw the cherubs and the flying chariot in the cloud of fire and lightning. If he was from the same town as those relocated by Sargon II, it would make sense for him to visit them, as they would have been his cousins.

A large number of Greek, Latin, Syriac, and Ge'ez manuscripts deviate on this name, with the largest alternate reading being Thebes. It is unclear if this was intended to represent Thebes in Egypt, or Greece, or another town in the mind of the translator. Thebes was a city in Greece at the time, however, the city later renamed Thebes in Egypt, was still known as was still known as Wôst (ⲓ).

The name Thêbês (ⲐHBHC) in the Codex Vaticanus, and Thebes (ⲐⲈBⲈC) in the Codex Alexandrinus, was also used as a translation for a name of a town in Canaan in the book of Judges chapter 9. The town's name is rendered as Tbs (תבץ) in the Aleppo Codex, and

TOBIT (SINAITICUS): CHAPTER 1 NOTES

Tēbēs (תֵּבֵץ) in the Leningrad Codex, and is generally accepted as being Tubas (طوباس) in the northern area of the modern Palestinian West Bank. As this is in the region where Tishbe (תִּשְׁבֶּ) was supposed to have been located, it is possible that both names refer to the same town.

4) Codex Sinaticus: Phogôr (φογωρ)

* Codex Monacensis (VL 130): Raphain
* Codex Corbeiensis (VL 150): Raphaim

Phogôr (Φογωρ) appears to be a variant spelling of Phagôr (Φαγὼρ), mentioned in the Septuagint's Joshua, and translated as Peor (פְּעוֹר) in the Masoretic Texts. As all three towns, Phogôr, Phagôr, and Peor are reported as being in the same general location, it does seem likely that this was a variant transliteration of Peor through Aramaic into Greek, and so the name Peor is used in this translation.

The Vetus Latina codices all use either Raphian or Raphiam, which are two alternate transliterations of the name Rəpāîm (רְפָאִים) from the Masoretic Texts. The term was transliterated as Raphaen (Ραφαιν) in the Septuagint, however, not in any surviving copies of the book of Tobit, suggesting the Vetus Latina manuscripts all descend from a non-Greek source text. The differences in transliteration between Raphain and Raphaim, used in different versions of the old Latin Tobit, may indicate two separate sources, as the word was spelled Rpåym (רפאים) in Hebrew and Rpåm (𐤓𐤐𐤀𐤌) in Phoenician, or Rpåyn (𐡓𐡐𐡀𐡉𐡍) in Aramaic and Raphain (Ραφαιν) in Coptic.

5) Codex Sinaiticus: oecou Dauid tou patros mou cae apo Ierousalêm (ΟΙΚΟΥ ΔΑΥΕΙΔ ΤΟΥ ΠΑΤΡΟΣ ΜΟΥ ΚΑΙ ΑΠΟ ΙΕΡΟΥΣΑΛΗΜ). Translation: house of David of my father and from Jerusalem

• Codex Vaticanus: oecou Ierosolymôn (ΟΙΚΟΥ ΙΕΡΟΣΟΛΥΜΩΝ). Translation: house of Jerusalem, temple in Jerusalem

The Codex Sinaiticus version is more political than the Vaticanus version, focused in the House of David, and the city of Jerusalem, instead of the temple specifically, although that is important too, and is referenced in the rest of the sentence in both versions. The focus on David is more commonly found in Aramaic texts than Hebrew, where the Kingdom of Judah was commonly referred to as the Kingdom of David.

6) Codex Sinaiticus: catascênôseôs (ΚΑΤΑΣΚΗΝΩΣΕΩΣ). Translation: camping place

This is most likely an attempt to translate 'tabernacle' into Greek via Aramaic, and so the more common term is used in this translation.

7) Codex Sinaiticus: theou (ΘΕΟΥ). Translation: god

• Codex Vaticanus: ypsistou (ΥΨΙΣΤΟΥ). Translation: highest

• Codex Monacensis (VL 130): dei. Translation: god

• Codex Sangermanensis 4 (VL 7): sanctificationis. Translation: sanctification

• Codex Bobbiensis (VL 135): sanctimonii. Translation: virtuousness

The temple in Jerusalem was commonly called the Temple of God, or occasionally, in some older Aramaic texts, Temple of the gods. It was rarely called the Temple of the Highest, which supports the Vaticanus version being redaction, but does not identify the era of the redaction. Early-Jewish texts from the Persian era did use the term Highest frequently, however, the Essenes also used the term, and the Tobian Jews most-likely would have had more contact with them than the Sadducees or Pharisees. Additionally, the early Aramaic-speaking Christians also used the term, so even Theodotion, who was Jewish, may have made the edit as late as circa 150 AD.

8) This final statement indicates that the original text must have been written before the first temple in Jerusalem was destroyed, in 586 BC.

9) The codices tell essentially the same story, however, the Codex Vaticanus version appears to be a Jewish redaction of the Codex Sinaiticus version. The setting of the event is during the life of Jeroboam II, the king of Samaria between circa 768 and 746 BC. His kingdom briefly conquered the Arameans of Damascus and Hama, creating the largest Israelite kingdom since the era of King David, and the largest that is known archaeologically, as evidence of the earlier United Kingdom of Israel has yet to be found. He was recorded as building shrines with icons of the calf-god in them, which outraged the prophets at the time, including Amos.

The Vaticanus's version of the verse in shorter, referring to the Baʻal calf, which is anachronistic, as the god Baʻal Hadad was not depicted as a calf, although he was depicted as having horns, like many Middle-eastern gods. Based on the archaeological evidence, such as the potshards discovered at Khirbet el-Kom and Kuntillet

TOBIT (SINAITICUS): CHAPTER 1 NOTES

Ajrud, the calf-god worshiped in Samaria circa 800 BC was Yahweh. The Sinaiticus version does not name the calf, however, does mention the town of Dan, which was where Jeroboam II built a shrine to the calf-god.

10) Codex Sinaiticus: prosêlytoes (ⲦⲢⲞⲤⲎⲀⲨⲦⲞⲒⲤ)

The Septuagint uses prosêlytoes (προσηλύτοις) in places where the Masoretic Texts has ger (גֵּר), meaning stranger, foreigner, or alien. It is generally accepted that this term referred to any foreigner that had converted to the Israelite religion(s), however, Tobit's inclusion of them in this verse implies they were seen as destitute within Israelite society at the time.

11) Greek: Midian (ⲘⲎⲆⲒⲀⲚ)

Media was the name of the land of the Medes, and ancient Iranian people who lived in northern Iran before the rise of the Persian Empire. The Medians were the allies of the Babylonians that jointly conquered the Assyrian Empire, a few decades after the story is set.

12) Codex Sinaiticus: Sennachirim (ⲤⲈⲚⲚⲀⲬⲎⲢⲒⲘ)

- Codex Venetus (LXX V): Chirim (ⲬⲈⲒⲢⲈⲒⲘ)

- Septuagint ms. 74: Rim (Ριμ)

- Septuagint ms. 314: Chirim (Χιριμ)

- Septuagint ms. 98: Senachrim (Σεναχρειμ)

- Septuagint ms. 318: Senachirim (Σεναχειρειμ)

- Septuagint ms. 106: Senachirim (Σεναχιρειμ)

- Septuagint ms. 130: Senachrim (Σεναχριμ)

TOBIT (SINAITICUS): CHAPTER 1 NOTES

- Septuagint ms. 71: Senachirim (Σεναχειριμ)
- Septuagint ms. 76: Senachirim (Σεναχιριμ)
- Septuagint ms. 402: Senacherim (Σεναχερειμ)
- Septuagint ms. 126: Senachechrim (Σεναχεχριμ)
- Septuagint ms. 319: Senachri (Σεναχρι)
- Septuagint ms. 46: Sennachrib (Σενναχρειβ)
- Septuagint ms. 44: Naxim (Ναχιμ)
- Sahidic manuscripts: Senakherim (Cєnаxєpιм)

King Sennacherib was the king of the Assyrian Empire between 705 and 681 BC. His reign was spent fighting a series of insurrections in Babylonia and Canaan. He also launched a punitive invasion of Elam, that virtually wiped out the nation. His campaigns in Canaan included laying siege to Jerusalem, which had previously been allied to Assyria.

13) Codex Sinaiticus: basileus tou ouranou (вλсιλєyc тоy оyρλnоy). Translation: king the vaulted-sky

- Codex Sangermanensis 4 (VL 7): deus. Translation: god
- Codex Monacensis (VL 130): dominus. Translation: lord

While this term can be interpreted as references to several gods in the region, the one most-likely intended was Ashur (✳𒐫𒈨𒄒), who under Sargon II's rule became known as Anshar (𒀭𒆜) meaning the 'whole sky.' Ashur was the king of the gods in the Assyrian pantheon since the mid-3rd-millennium BC, however, during Sargon II's rule also became a sky-god.

14) This was the year 681 BC, when Sennacherib was killed by his sons Arda-Mulissu and Nabu-shar-usur. This is calculated by Assyriologists as having taken place on 20 October, meaning Tobit would have gone into hiding sometime in mid-September. The Codex Vaticanus reads 'less than 50 days.'

15) Codex Sinaiticus: Ararat (ⲁⲣⲁⲣⲁⲧ)

- Codex Vaticanus: Ararath (ⲁⲣⲁⲣⲁⲑ)

- Sahidic manuscripts: Ararad (ⲁ̀ⲣⲁⲣⲁⲁ)

The Assyrian records record the princes as retreating to the Kingdom of ᵏᵘʳUrartu (𒆳𒌕) in the Armenian Highlands. The name of this country was recorded as Ararat (אֲרָרַט) in Hebrew, and Urartu (Ուրարտու) in Armenian. The Greek name is a transliteration of the Hebrew name, however, the more common historical name of Urartu is used in this translation.

16) Codex Sinaiticus: Sacherdonos (ⲥⲁⲭⲉⲣⲁⲟⲛⲟⲥ)

- Codex Alexandrinus: Sacherdan (ⲥⲁⲭⲉⲣⲁⲁⲛ)

- Codex Venetus: Nacherdonos (ⲛⲁⲭⲉⲣⲁⲟⲛⲟⲥ)

- Septuagint ms. 74: Sacherdônos (Σαχερδωνος)

- Septuagint ms. 314: Sacherdon (Σαχερδον)

- Septuagint ms. 538: Sacherdôn (Σαχερδων)

- Septuagint ms. 64: Sarchedonos (Σαρχεδονοσ)

- Septuagint ms. 46: Sachedôr (Σαχεδωρ)

- Septuagint ms. 248: Acherdonos (Αχερδονος)

- Septuagint ms. 98: Achirdônos (Αχειρδωνος)

- Septuagint ms. 542: Nachordanos (Ναχορδανος)

- Sahidic manuscripts: Sakherdônias (Сахердωνιас)

- Armenian Bible: Asordan (Ասորդւււ)

- Codex Codex Corbeiensis (VL 150): Archedonassar

- Codex Monacensis (VL 130): Arcedonossar

- Codex Bobbiensis (VL 135): Nachoda ,

- Codex Complutensis 1 (VL 109): Natordan

Esarhaddon is the more common name of King Aššur-Aḫa-Iddina, Sennacherib's youngest son and heir. The name Esarhaddon is derived from the Latin Hazor Haddan, which was in turn derived from the Greek Asarchaddon (Ασαρχαδδων), which was used in direct translations from Assyrian texts. Sacherdonos (Σαχερδονος) appears to be a Greek transliteration of the Aramaic version of his name.

17) Codex Sinaiticus: Achicharon (ΑΧΙΧΑΡΟΝ)

- Codex Vaticanus: Achiacharon (ΑΧΙΑΧΑΡΟΝ)

- Septuagint ms. 107: Achiachar (Αχιαχαρ)

- Vetus Latina manuscripts: Achicarum

This name is generally translated as Ahikar, the famous, possibly fictional hero of the Words of Ahikar, the oldest known Jewish or Samaritan text to survive intact to the present. The oldest copy found to date is from around 500 BC, a couple of centuries older than the oldest of the Dead Sea Scrolls. Tobit does allude to the story of Ahikar's betrayal by his nephew, which is found in the Words of Ahikar, and it is accepted that this was a reference to that Ahikar, however, both stories are also regarded as fiction by most scholars, and so the authors may have been the same person.

It is also possible that both books began as historical texts that then became fictionalized, however, if additional elements were added, they must have been added to the Words of Ahikar before the oldest surviving copy, from circa 500 BC. As both Ahikar and Tobit are reported to have lived circa 700 BC, this is not a great deal of time for the books to have been altered, however, as all books were copied by hand at the time, it is possible that the scribes felt a more fantastic version of the tales of these two men's lives would sell better.

Tobit (Sinaiticus): Chapter 2

King Esarhaddon restored to me my home, and this afforded my wife Hannah, and my son Tobiah to prepare a Pentecost feast, which is the holy feast of the seven weeks, there was a good breakfast prepared for me, in which I sat down to eat., and he sat next to me at the table

When I sat down and saw the abundance of fish on the table, I said to Tobiah my son, "Child, walk around and look for an indigent brother who is captive in Nineveh, who remembers God[1] in his heart, and bring him to eat with me. I'll wait for you to return."

Then Tobiah went out to look for an indigent brother of ours, but when he returned he called out, "Father."

I answered, "Here I am."

He stated, "Father, one of our nation is murdered, and is throw down in the marketplace, and is laying there right now!"

Then I jumped to leave before I had tasted any of it, and retrieved him from the square and placed him in a shed until the sun sank, and then I buried him. Then I returned, and bathed myself, and ate my food after morning, remembering the words of the prophet of Amos[2] who said in Bethel, "Your feasts will be turned into mourning, and all your songs into lamentations." I wept, and after the sunset, I went and dug a grave and buried him.

Those near me laughed at me, saying, "He's not afraid any longer. Already he has been searched for to be executed for this thing and ran away, and again he buries their dead."

The same night I returned from bathing, I entered my courtyard to sleep, and despite the walls of my courtyard, my face was uncovered because of the heat. I did not know that there were sparrows inside with me, and while I was gazing up, they defecated into my eyes, causing a warm white film. I went to the physicians to be cured, but after many ointments and many medicines, I was still going blind, and my eyes continued to have white film until I was quite blind, and I was weak and without eyes for four years.

All of my brothers grieved for me, and Ahikar supported me for two years before he went to Elam.[3] Eventually Hannah, my wife, took inside work with women.

Once when the lord of the place paid her, he gave the salary on the seventh of Dystrus,[4] when she took down the loom beam,[5] the lord sent her off with her regular wages and also gave her a goat kid for the house. When she returned with the kid, the first time it bleated, I called her and I asked, "Where did this kid come from. Did you steal it? Return it quickly as the lord is powerful, and we have never eaten anything stolen."

She replied to me, "It was given as a gift in addition to my wages."

I did not believe her and commanded her to return it to its owner, and I was angry because of it, but she replied to me, "What about your charitable works and your just deeds? All your works are known!"

Tobit (Sinaiticus): Chapter 2 Notes

1) Codex Sinaiticus: êlê (ΗΛΗ)

• Codex Vaticanus: cyriou (ΚΥΡΙΟΥ). Translation: lord (main, chief, dominant, master)

The Sinaiticus version of Tobit includes a direct Greek transliteration of the Aramaic elah (𐡀𐡋𐡄) meaning 'god,' which proves the translators were working off of an Aramaic source-text.

2) The prophet Amos was active in Samaria and Judah between 760 and 755 BC, and is believed to have died in 745 BC, about 66 years before this event.

3) Codex Sinaiticus: Elymaeda (ΕΛΥΜΑΙΔΑ)

• Codex Vaticanus: Ellymaeda (ΕΛΛΥΜΑΙΔΑ)

• Septuagint ms. 107: Elimaeda (*Ελιμαιδα*)

• Septuagint ms. 98: Eloemaeda (*Ελοιμαιδα*)

• Septuagint ms. 71: Elemaeda (*Ελεμαιδα*)

• Septuagint ms. 126: Lymaeda (*Λυμαιδα*)

• Codex Corbeiensis (VL 150): Limaidam

• Codex Monacensis (VL 130): Lymaidem

Haltamti (𒀸𒁃𒉺𒋫) was a major nation in southern modern Iran, until it was virtually destroyed by the kings of Assyria in the 7th-century BC. The Babylonian name of the land was Elamma[ki] (𒉏𒈠𒆠), which was adopted into Hebrew as Elam (עֵילָם) and Greek as Elám (Ελάμ), ultimately resulting in the modern English name Elam. The conflict in question is likely the events near the beginning of Esarhaddon's rule, when an ethnically Elamite Assyrian governor named Nabu-zer-kitti-lišir in southern Babylonia revolted against Assyrian rule and besieged Ur. Esarhaddon's army defeated Nabu-zer-kitti-lišir, and he fled to Elam, where he was ultimately captured and executed.

4) Codex Sinaiticus: Dystrou (ⲆⲨⲤⲦⲢⲞⲨ). Translation: Dystrus

Dystrus was the fifth month of the ancient Macedonian calendar, and then the corresponding month in the Seleucid calendar, developed after General Seleucus I Nicator's reconquest of Babylon in 312 BC. The Seleucid calendar was in use for centuries in the Middle East, well into the Christian Era in some regions, however, was never in use in Egypt, where the Ptolemy's adopted the Egyptian Civil Calendar, and renamed the months to correspond with the Athenian calendar. This indicates that the Sinaiticus version of Tobit was not translated in Alexandria, but somewhere in the Seleucid Empire, which included most of the territory of modern Iran, Iraq, Syria, Lebanon. Afghanistan, Turkmenistan, Pakistan, Uzbekistan, and Turkey, at their height. It is likely that it was adopted by the editor of the Codex Sinaiticus as it appears to be an older and superior copy of Tobit, nevertheless, almost certainly not the translation made in Alexandria.

5) Codex Sinaiticus: istos (ⲓⲤⲦⲞⲤ). Translation: mast (or shinbone, beam or a loom, loom, web of a loom)

Unlike the modern loom, in the ancient Greek looms had upright beams.

Tobit (Sinaiticus): Chapter 3

I became depressed and sighed, and cried, and after sighing, I prayed, "Sydyk exists![1] Lord, all your works are fair, and all your ways are mercy and truth, and you judge truly and justly for ages. Now, remember me, and look down on me. Don't punish me for my sins and ignorance, and the sins of my fathers, who have sinned before you, and did not obey your commandments, and broke your covenant with us, therefore you have given us as captives, and to death, and as a parable of humbleness and an insult before all the nations among whom we are scattered. Now, your judgments are many and true. Deal with me according to my sins and my forefathers' because we have not kept your commandments, nor have walked in truth before you.

Now, if it is acceptable to you take my spirit from me, and remove me from the face of the Earth, and make me dirt rather than life, as I am insulted and lied to, and have many regrets. Lord, command that I may be released from my duties, and taken to the place of ages. Don't turn your face away from me."

On the day this happened, Sarah the daughter of Raguel in the city of Ecbatana[2] in Media, overheard an insult from a child, and a reproach against her father, because she was given to husbands seven times, and

Asmodeus[3] the cunning demon[4] had killed them before she was with them in the way of women.

Then the children said, "You have killed your man! Already you were given seven husbands, and you were not called by any of their names. Why do you whip us because of these men? If they are dead, go be with them, and let us not see either a son or daughter from you for ages."

On that day, she was depressed in the mind, and cried, and got up and went upstairs and was considering hanging herself, but reconsidered, and said, "I could never do this to my father. If a family exists and their only daughter hanged herself, it will be a reproach, and I will bring his old age with sadness to Hades.[5] It would be better if I was not strangled, but I lack a husband, and therefore am insulted and mocked all my life."

At that time she held her hands up to the window, and said, "Bless you God, and blessed is your name for ages. Let all praise you forever, and your projects in their ages. Now, I turn I my face and my eyes and look up and say, 'Take me out of the earth, that I may no longer hear the reproach.' You know, Lord,[6] that I am pure from all sin with a man, and that I never defiled my name, or the name of my father, in the land of my captivity. I am the only daughter of my father, and he has no other child to be his heir, nor a brother, nor any near relative to whom I may offer myself to as a wife. My seven husbands are already dead, and why do I exist? I don't expect to have a family, and should die, Lord, now, hear my insults."

At that time, both prayers were heard before the glory of God, and he sent Raphael[7] to heal the two, to Tobit to destroy the white film from his eyes, so that he may perceive with his eyes the light of God, and to Sarah, for Raphael to give to her Tobiah the son of Tobit as a wife, and to drive Asmodeus the cunning demon from her, because she belonged to Tobiah by right of inheritance. Tobit returned into his house from of courtyard, and Sarah of Raguel descended from the upper floor.

Tobit (Sinaiticus): Chapter 3 Notes

1) Codex Sinaiticus: Dicaeos i (ⲇⲓⲕⲁⲓⲟⲥⲉ). Translation: Justice exists, fairness exists

The name Dicaeos (Δίκαιος) was repeatedly used in the books of prophecy of the Septuagint were the word ṣdq (צדק) is used in the Masoretic Texts. Both words translate as 'justice' or 'fairness,' however, the term was also the name of the Canaanite and early-Israelite god of Justice, Sydyk, which also became the Hebrew name of the Roman god Jupiter, and continues to be the Hebrew name for the planet Jupiter. As this is a statement at the beginning of a prayer, 'Dicaeos exists,' it seems more likely that Tobit was addressing the then-popular Israelite god Sydyk, than making a generic declaration, and so 'Sydyk exists' is used in this translation. In the Greek era, Sydyk was worshiped by the Hassidian sect of Judahites, who migrated to northern Italy and Dalmatia during the Maccabean Revolt.

2) Codex Sinaiticus: Ekbatanois (ⲉⲕⲃⲁⲧⲁⲛⲟⲓⲥ)

- Septuagint ms. 243: Ecbasanoes (Εκβασανοις)

- Codex Complutensis 1 (VL 109): Bethanis

- Ge'ez manuscripts: Bathani (በታኒ)

Ecbatana was the capital of the Median Empire, and later the summer capital of the Persian Empire. Its name translates in old Persian as 'the place of gathering.'

3) Codex Sinaiticus: Asmodeos (ⲁⲥⲙⲟⲇⲉⲟⲥ)

- Codex Vaticanus: Asmodaus (ⲁⲥⲙⲟⲇⲁⲩⲥ)

- Septuagint ms. 319: Asmodeus (Ἀσμοδεὺς)

- Septuagint ms. 46: Asmodaeon (Ἀσμοδαιον)

- Codex Bobbiensis (VL 135): Asmadeum

- Codex Complutensis 1 (VL 109): Nasbodeus

Asmodeus is a Jewish and Samaritan demon, adopted from the Zoroastrian faith. The name is derived from the Avestan aēšəma daēuua (ﺳﻮ)ﻳﻮﺳﻮ و ﺳﻮﻳﻮﺳ؟ﺳﻮ6), which translates as wrath-demon. At the time, Zoroastrianism was one of the religions practiced in Media.

4) Codex Sinaiticus: to daemonion to ponêron (ⲦⲞ ⲆⲀⲒⲘⲞⲚⲒⲞⲚ ⲦⲞ ⲠⲞⲚⲎⲢⲞⲚ). Translation: the demon (or divine, lesser god, powerful spirit) the wrathful (or painful, oppressive, grievous)

- Codex Vaticanus: to ponêron daemonion (ⲦⲞ ⲠⲞⲚⲎⲢⲞⲚ ⲆⲀⲒⲘⲞⲚⲒⲞⲚ). Translation: the wrathful (or painful, oppressive, grievous) demon (or divine, lesser god, powerful spirit)

The Greek term has many interpretations, and at its core relates to something powerful. As the being in question was a Zoroastrian demon, the original term used in the Aramaic text was likely and Aramaic translation of the Avestan term aēšəma daēuua (ﺳﻮ)ﻳﻮﺳﻮ و ﺳﻮﻳﻮﺳ؟ﺳﻮ6), which translates as 'wrath demon.'

5) Codex Sinaiticus: aidou (ⲀⲒⲆⲞⲨ). Translation: Hades

6) Codex Sinaiticus: despota (ⲆⲈⲤⲠⲞⲦⲀ). Translation: despot (or tyrant, lord, bishop, master, ruler)

- Codex Vaticanus: cyrie (ⲔⲨⲢⲒⲈ). Translation: lord (or main, chief, dominant, master)

As both despota and cyrie are used in the Septuagint as translations of a word meaning Lord, it is unlikely that either of the two codices was based on the other, as there would have been no reason to replace one word with the other. This points to two separate translations of the Book of Tobit into Greek from Aramaic.

7) Codex Sinaiticus: Rafail (ⲣⲁⲫⲁⲏⲗ)

• Codex Vaticanus: megalou Raphaêl (ⲙⲉⲅⲁⲗⲟⲩⲣⲁⲫⲁⲏⲗ). Translation: great Raphael

• Septuagint ms. 126: megalou Theos cae apestile Cyrios Raphaêl ton angelon autou (μεγαλου Θεος και απεστειλε Κυριος Ραφαηλ τον αγγελον αυτου). Translation: great god and sent Lord Raphael the messenger himself

• Septuagint ms. 311: megalou apestal Raphaêl (μεγαλου απεσταλ Ραφαηλ). Translation: great apostle Raphael

• Codex Bobbiensis (VL 135): Raphael angelus. Translation: Raphael angel

Raphael was a messenger in some Jewish sects and later adopted by Christians and Muslims. Raphael only appears in the books of Tobit and Enoch (1st Enoch). Both seem to have been important to the Essen community later, and neither was of interest to the Pharisees or Sadducees. As Josephus claimed the Essenes considered themselves to be descents of the ancient Canaanites, it is plausible that this name started as a reference to the healing god (Rapha El), who was worshiped in Canaan before the Israelites conquered the Canaanites.

Tobit (Sinaiticus): Chapter 4

On that day, Tobit remembered the silver that he had loaned to Gabael in Ray[1] in Media, and said in his heart, "I have wished for death, no! I will call for my son Tobiah, so I can tell him about the silver before I die."

He called Tobiah his son, and when he came to his side, he said, "Bury me honorably, and support your mother, and don't abandon her all the days of your life, and do that which is acceptable to her, and do not grieve her spirit ever. Remember, my son, that she saw many dangers for you when you were in her womb, and when she is dead, bury her next to me in the same grave."

"My son, be mindful of our Lord all your days and don't let your will be set to sin or to transgress his commandments. Do correctly all your life, and don't follow the ways of dishonesty. If you deal honestly, your business will prosper and you will succeed. Give to charities from your property. The Lord gives to those that follow the noble counsel and the will of the Lord. Now, child, I signify for our family, that I placed ten talents of silver with Gabael, the son of Gabri in Ray in Media."

Don't be afraid, my son, that we are made poor, for you have much honest wealth, if you fear God, and flee from all sin, and do that which is pleasing in the sight of Lord your god.

Tobit (Sinaiticus): Chapter 4 Notes

1) Codex Sinaiticus: Argoes (Ⲁⲣⲅⲟⲓⲥ)

• Codex Vaticanus: Ragoes (ⲣⲀⲅⲟⲓⲥ)

• Septuagint manuscript 318: Ragoê (Ραγοη)

• Septuagint manuscript 670: Raga (Ραγα)

• Septuagint manuscript 319: Rassois (Ρασσοις)

• Septuagint manuscript 64: Agrois (Αγροις)

This is accepted as the Greek name of Ray (ری), an ancient city near Tehran in Iran. It is regarded as the oldest continuously inhabited city in Tehran Province, dating back to the Median Empire. The Greek name used in this book is likely a transliteration of the Aramaic name of the era, itself transliterated from the Assyrian name Raga (𒂍𒉏𒁹𒈜𒀀𒋫). The older Elamite name was Rakkaan (𒁹𒉿𒀯), while the later Old Persian name was Ragae (𒂍𒈫𒊺).

Tobit (Sinaiticus): Chapter 5

Then Tobiah answered Tobit his father, "Everything, you have told me I will do, father. But how can I receive the silver, seeing I do not know him? What token can he see and believe me and give me the silver? Also, I don't know the roads of Media to travel there."

Then Tobit responded and said to Tobiah his son, "This is the document he gave me, a handwritten agreement made between the two of us. Each took a copy, when I left the silver there, more than twenty years ago,[1] so request the silver. And now, child, find a trustworthy man who will travel with you, and pay him to travel to the east, and carry the silver."

Tobiah went out to search for a man to travel with him to Media who knew the roads, and while he was out happened upon Raphael the messenger,[2] standing across from him, and he did not know that he was a messenger of God, and he asked him, "Who are you, young man?"

He asked him, "From the Israelites, your brothers. I came here looking for work."

He asked him, "Do you know the roads that go to Media?"

He answered, "Yes, I have traveled there often, and am experienced and knowledgeable of all the roads. Also, I have traveled in Media and lodged near Gabael our brother's house in Ray in Media, and it is only two days travel along the road from Ecbatana to Ray and lies in the mountains."

He asked, "Wait for me, young man, until I go to get my father's advice, since I need someone to travel with me, and my family will pay you."

He replied to him, "I'll wait, only don't take long."

Tobiah went to tell Tobit his father, and said, "I found a man from among our brothers, the Israelites."

He replied, "Call this man to me, so I may know of what tribe he is, and whether he is a trustworthy man to travel with you, child."

So Tobiah went and called him, saying, "Young man, my father calls you in."

He went to him, and spoke with Tobit, saying, "Amen[3] bring you much joy!"

Tobit replied to him, "What do I have to be happy about? I am a feeble man, blind, and unable to see the light of the sky,[4] but I stand in the shadow of death, to be mocked by the light. I am the living dead. I hear the voice of men, but I cannot see them."

He replied, "Have courage, God may heal you. Have courage."

Tobit replied to him, "Tobiah my son wants to travel to Media. If you are capable of traveling with him leading him, my family will pay you, brother."

He replied, "I am capable of traveling with him. I am knowledgeable of all the roads, and have often gone to Media, passing through the fields and the mountains. I know all the roads.

He asked him, "Brother, who is your father, and which tribe are you from? Tell me, brother."

He answered, "What do you need a tribe for?"

He said to him, I want to know truthfully, who are you brother, and what is your name?"

He answered him, "I am Azariah of the great Hananiah, your brother."

He replied, "Greetings and welcome, brother. Don't be angry brother, because I demanded to know the truth of who your father was, and you, child, are from a good and noble family. I know Hananiah and Nathan,[5] the two sons of the great Shemaiah and they accompanied me in Jerusalem, and they worshiped with me there, and they did not sin. Your brothers are good and your people are good, your are from a good root. Come and celebrate."

And he offered, "I will pay you a beka[6] each day, and costs equal to my son's, and you will travel with my son, and also my family will add a bonus."

He replied, "I will travel with him and don't be afraid, he will be safe departing, and safely returned to you because the roads are safe."

He said to him, "Amen bless you, brother," and he said to his son, "Child, prepare for the road, and leave with this brother, and the god in the sky[7] will protect you on the way there and return you to me safely, and his messenger accompanying you will protect you, child."

As he set out on the road and said goodbye to his father and his mother, Tobit said, "Travel safely."

His mother wept and said to Tobit "Why have you sent away my child? Is he not the staff of our hand, going in and out before us? Do not be greedy to add silver to silver, but let it be considered as nothing in comparison to our child, Amen! For that which the Lord has given us to live with is enough for us."

He replied to her, "Don't worry, he will travel safely, and safely return to us, and your eyes will see him in the future when he returns safely. There is no reason to be fearful about it sister, as the good messenger will keep him company, and his journey will be prosperous, and he will return safe," and so she stopped crying.

Tobit (Sinaiticus): Chapter 5 Notes

1) This reference to twenty years is consistent with Tobit's claims to have traveled to Media for King Sargon II (Ενεμεσσαρου), and to be sending his son there again during the time of King Esarhaddon (Σαχερδονος). Sargon II ruled between 722 and 705 BC, and Esarhaddon ruled between 681 and 669 BC. If the roads were closed during at least some of the reign of Sennacherib (Σενναχηριμ), as previously stated, then that would have been between 705 and 681 BC, a time period of 24 years.

Most of Sennacherib's reign was focused on suppressing local rebellions, including a major rebellion in Babylonia backed by Elam. It is unclear what the situation was with Media at the time as there are few records, however, Media did back the later Babylonian rebellion that toppled the Assyrian Empire in 612 BC, and so it is plausible they had backed the Babylonian rebellion in 689 BC as well.

2) Codex Sinaiticus: angelos tou theou (ᴀггєλocτoʏθєoʏ). Translation: messenger of the god

- Codex Vaticanus: angelos (ᴀггєλoc). Translation: messenger

- Septuagint ms. 236: angelon (αγγελον). Translation: messenger

- Septuagint ms. 71: angelos Cyriou (αγγελος Κυριου). Translation: messenger of Lord

3) Codex Sinaiticus: Genoeto (гєɴoιтo)

- Septuagint ms. 71: Genêtae (Γενηται)

The Greek term Genoeto (Γένοιτο) is used in the Septuagint as a translation of the word that is represented in the Masoretic texts as

Amen (אָמֵן), and therefore restored in this translation, however, in the Codex Sinaiticus' version of Tobit, it is used as a proper name, and in chapter 10 it is referred to as God's great name, suggesting that the Samaritans viewed Amen the Egyptian sun-god as another version of Shemesh, the Israelite sun-god prior to King Josiah's banning the worship of Shemesh circa 625 BC.

4) Codex Sinaiticus: ouranou (ΟΥΡΑΝΟΥ). Translation: vaulted-sky

As the original term was in Aramaic, but it is unclear whether it was Shamayim or Bethel, the generic translation of 'sky' is used.

5) Codex Sinaiticus: Nathan (ΝΑΘΑΝ)

• Codex Vaticanus: Iathan (ΙΑΘΑΝ)

• Septuagint ms. 319: Nathanian (Ναθανιαν)

• Codex Sangermanensis 4: Athaniam

Iathan is almost certainly a misspelling of Nathan, as it is only known from the books of Tobit. This suggests that even though the Sinaiticus Codex version of Tobit has many of what appear to be spelling errors in the Greek text if one assumes a Koine origin, the text was copied correctly by the scribes. The Sinaiticus text contains many words that were more common in the Ionic dialect than the Attic, which was the ancestral-dialect of Koine, suggesting that the errors may have simply been Ionic spelling variation.

6) Codex Sinaiticus: drachmên (ΔΡΑΧΜΗΝ)

• Codex Corbeiensis (VL 150): didragmam

The drachma was a Greek coin used from around 1100 BC, worth approximately 4.3 grams of silver. The name drachma was used in the Septuagint as a translation for the beka (בֶּקַע), was the half-shekel measurement used in ancient Canaan. As 'drachma' was the Greek translation of beka, the term beka is restored.

7) Codex Sinaiticus: theos o en tô ouranô (ⲐⲈⲞⲤ Ⲟ ⲈⲚ ⲦⲰ ⲞⲨⲢⲀⲚⲰ). Translation: god that is the Uranus (or sky)

• Codex Vaticanus: ouranô oecôn theos (ⲞⲨⲢⲀⲚⲰⲞⲒⲔⲰⲚ ⲐⲈⲞⲤ). Translation: Uranus (or sky) house god

The proper name of Uranus is used in both versions, however, could not have been in the Aramaic source text the Greeks used. The name is found in both versions of Tobit, and so it is likely that it was in the original Greek translations. The Vaticanus version clearly points to the Aramaic source as referring to Bytål (𐤁𐤉𐤕𐤀𐤋), the Canaanite and early-Israelite sky-god, however, the Sinaiticus is more generic in its translation of the source.

According to both the prophet Jeremiah, who was present for the destruction of Jerusalem, and settled with the Israelite refugees in southern Egypt, as well as the archaeological evidence in southern Egypt, the Israelite refugees continued worshiping Bytål, along with Yahw and Anat until at least the Persian era. Nevertheless, this manuscript is not clear on which sky-god is being addressed, possibly because the Greeks had just conquered the Persians, and Alexander was in the process of exterminating the Zoroastrian magi, and the translator wanted the Greek reader of the text to infer the god in the sky was Zeus. In any event, the god in question was likely Bytål/Bethel/Baitylos or Shamayim/Anu, as these gods were widely worshiped by the Samaritans before King Jeroboam II decided everyone should worship the calf-god Yahweh, which Tobit had rejected.

Tobit (Sinaiticus): Chapter 6

They traveled, the young man and the messenger with him, and his dog also walked alongside him. They traveled together until one night when they camped along the bank of the Tigris River. The young man went down to wash his feet in the Tigris River, and a huge fish came out of the water intending to bite off the foot of the young man, but the messenger called out to the young man, "Avoid the fish, and catch it!"

The young man was strong and dragged the fish up onto the land, and the messenger stated, "Cut up the fish, and remove the bile, and the heart, and the liver, and keep the guts on yourself. There are useful medicines[1] that can be made from the bile, and the heart and the liver, but cook the fish eat it, and salt the rest to eat on the road."

Then they continued traveling together on the road to Ecbatana, and the young man asked the messenger, "Azariah, brother, what medicine is made from the heart and the liver and the bile of the fish?"

He answered him, "The heart and the liver of the fish can be smoked in front of a man or woman who is possessed with a demon or destructive spirit,[2] and it will leave its possessee, and not return to him for ages, and the bile can be used to anoint the eyes of a man with white film formed on them, and the white film will be healed."

When they had crossed into Media and were approaching Ecbatana, Raphael said to Tobiah, the young man, "Brother."

He replied, "I'm here."

He stated, "We will lodge with Raguel tonight, who is your male relative and has a daughter named Sarah, and no other son or daughter exists other than Sarah alone. You are her kin and so you can inherit everything through her. The claim through her father's family justifies the inheritance, and the girl is wise and courageous, and very good, and her father is good."

He continued, "It is justified you take her. Hear me, brother, and speak to her father about the girl tonight, so that you may take her as your bride when you return from Ray, and can be wed to her, and know that Raguel will not refuse you from being married, without incurring death by going against the judgment of the book of Moses. Know that you will inherit, if you take his daughter, before all other people. Now, listen to me brother, and talk about the girl tonight, and make an agreement with the family, so when you return from Ray, we may take her back to your home."

Then Tobiah replied to Raphael, "Azariah, brother, I heard that she has already been given to seven men, who died in the bride-chamber[3] the night of their marriage to her. They are now dead, and I heard it said that a demon killed them, and now I'm afraid, not of her injustice, but of that who wishes to be with her, it may murder me. I am my father's only child, and I am afraid, I will die, and bring my father's and my mother's life to the grave with sorrow because of me, for they have no other son to bury them."

Then he replied to him, "Don't you remember the commands which your father gave you, that you should marry a wife of your own family? Now, listen to me, brother, and don't be concerned about the demon but marry her, and know that tonight she will be given you in marriage. When you enter the bride-chamber, take the liver of the fish, and its heart and add them to the ashes on the incense burners, and a strong odor will emerge, and when the demon smells it will flee and not bother her again forever."

Tobit (Sinaiticus): Chapter 6 Notes

1) Codex Sinaiticus: pharmacon (ϕⲀⲢⲘⲀⲔⲞⲚ). Translation: medicine (or drug, potion, remedy)

- Septuagint ms. 319: pharmaca (φαρμακα). Translation: medicine (or drug, potion, poison)

- Codex Complutensis 1 (VL 109): medicamenta. Translation: medicines (or drugs, remedies)

2) Codex Sinaiticus: daimoniou ê pneumatos ponêrou (ⲆⲀⲓⲘⲞⲚⲓⲞⲨ Ⲏ ⲠⲚⲈⲨⲘⲀⲦⲞⲤ ⲠⲞⲚⲎⲢⲞⲨ). Translation: demon (or lesser god, powerful spirit, divinity) or (or as) spirit (or wind, breath, life, air, angel) destructive (or painful, grievous)

- Codex Vaticanus: daemonion ê paneuma ponêron (ⲆⲀⲓⲘⲞⲚⲓⲞⲚⲎⲠⲀⲚⲈⲨⲘⲀⲠⲞⲚⲎⲢⲞⲚ). Translation: demon (or lesser god, powerful spirit, divinity) or (or as) spirit (or wind, breath, life, air, angel) destructive (or painful, grievous)

- Septuagint manuscript 71: daemonion (δαιμονιον). Translation: demon (or lesser god, powerful spirit, divinity)

The phrase appears to originate in the Zoroastrian terms daeva (ﻭ_ﺟﻮ))ﺟﻮ), meaning 'demon,' and Angra Mainyu (ﺟﺮﻳﺎ6·ﺟﻠﻳﺮﺟ), meaning 'destructive spirit.'

3) Codex Sinaiticus: nymphôn (ⲚⲨⲘϕⲱⲚ). Translation: nuptial apartment

- Septuagint ms. 319: nymphôni (νυμφωνι). Translation: nuptial apartment

- Codex Complutensis 1 (VL 109): nuptias. Translation: weddings

The Greek word nymphôn (νυμφων) referred to a room in which marriages were consummated, much like a modern honeymoon suit, although more formal.

Tobit (Sinaiticus): Chapter 7

When they arrived in Ecbatana, he stated, "Azariah, brother, lead me straight to Raguel our brother," and he led him to Raguel's house, and they found him sitting at the door to his courtyard.

He welcomed them, saying, "Greetings brothers," and welcomed them into his house.

Edna, his wife asked, "How much does this young man look like my cousin Tobit!" and then Edna asked them, "From where are you, brothers?"

They answered, "We are of the Naphtalites who were taken captives to Nineveh."

Then they asked them, "Do you know Tobit our relative?"

They answered, "We know him."

Then they asked, "Is he well?"

They answered, "Alive, and in good health," and Tobiah added, "he is my father."

Then Raguel leaped up, and kissed him, and wept. He said to him, "Amen bless you, child. You are of a kind and noble father! Oh, he suffers badly! That blind man, honest, but a source of great pity." He hugged Tobiah their brother around the neck and wept, and Edna his wife, and Sarah their daughter also wept. Nevertheless, they welcomed them cheerfully into their house, and they bathed and cleaned their feet.

Then make a meal, and Tobiah said to Raphael, "Azariah, brother, talk to Raguel about me and Sarah, my sister."

Raguel listened to the reasoning and said to the young man, "Eat and drink, be celebrate tonight young man, as no other man will take Sarah my daughter, except you, brother. I will not give her to any man but you, as you are my very nearest and most intimate family, child. I have engaged her to seven men, brother, and everyone died on his wedding night when led into the bride-chamber. Now, child, eat and drink, and the Lord will work through you."

Tobiah replied, "I will not eat or drink anything here until you come to an agreement with me."

Raguel said, "Agreed, Then take her from now on according to our custom, as you are her cousin, and she is yours, and the merciful God gave you good success in all things."

Then he called his daughter Sarah, and she came to her father, and he took her by the hand, and gave her to Tobiah as a wife, saying, "Look, I give her to your family according to the laws of the book of Moses, as Shamayim[1] ordered I give her to you. Take her, the sister is yours from now on brother. She is your sister, whom I give you today and for the ages, and the Lord of the sky will bless you, child, tonight, and to be fruitful as long and who have mercy and peace."

Raguel called Sarah his daughter to him, and she came, and he took her hand and gave her to him stating, "Take care of her according to our customs, and the laws written in the book of Moses, I hereby give her to you as a wife. Take her back to your father safely, and may the god Shamayim[2] bless you and give you peace."

Her mother called her and said, "Bring the book," and she wrote, 'We give her to him as a wife according to the judgments of the law of Moses,' and they began to eat and drink.

Raguel called to Edna his wife, and said, "Sister, prepare the bridal-chamber, and take them there."

She walked to the bridal-chamber and said, "Take her in," and wept with her, and said, "Be courageous daughter, the Lord Shamayim will grant you joy instead of sorrow. Be courageous daughter," and she left.

Tobit (Sinaiticus): Chapter 7 Notes

1) Codex Sinaiticus: Ouranou (ουρανου). Translation: Uranus (or vaulted-sky)

In this sentence Ouranou (Οὐρανου) is being used as a proper name. As this is the Greek term for both Uranus, and the vaulted-sky that covered the world in the view of most of the Classical philosophers, the Hebrew term Shamayim is used, which is both the Israelite version of Uranus: the god Shamayim (שָׁמַיִם), and the Hebrew term for the vaulted-sky. The name Shamayim was used many times in the Masoretic Texts, and his worship was banned in Judah by King Josiah circa 625 BC.

2) Codex Sinaiticus: o cyrios tou ourano (OKYPIOCTOY OYPANO). Translation: the lord the vaulted-sky

• Codex Vaticanus: o theos tou ouranou (OΘEOCTOY OYPANOY). Translation: the god the vaulted-sky

• Codex Alexandrinus: o cyrios tou ourano (O ΘEOC TOY OYPANO TEKNA). Translation: the god of the vaulted-sky's child (or descendant)

• Septuagint manuscript 107: ho cyrios Theos tou ouranou (ὁ κύριος Θεὸς τοῦ οὐρανοῦ). Translation: the lord God of the sky

The vaulted-sky (Οὐρανοῦ) of early Greek cosmology was based on, or very similar to, the Shamayim of the ancient Canaanite and Israelite religions. The Shamayim was the first thing created in Genesis, right before Eretz (Earth).

Tobit (Sinaiticus): Chapter 8

After they had entered into the bridal-chamber, and eaten and drank, and they wanted to sleep, the young man led her into the bed room. Tobiah remembered the words of Raphael, and took the liver of the fish, and its heart from the pouch, which he was carrying, and added it to the incense ash. The odor of the fish lingered, and the demon tried to flee to the region of Egypt, but Raphael moved quickly and caught it and tied its feet together and immediately bound it in shackles, and then exited the door to the bridal-chamber.

Tobiah rose from the bed, and said, "Sister, get up, and let's pray together to our Lord to give us mercy and salvation."

They arose and began to pray in order to bring themselves salvation. They prayed, "Blessed are you, God of our fathers, and blessed is your name in all ages and generations. Praise Shamayim,[1] and your house in all ages. You created Adam and created as a helper Eve[2] his wife, and from the two of them descended all the people, and you said that it is not good that the man is alone, and you created a helper for him of his own kind. Now, I do not take my sister like a prostitute, but we come together in honesty and I will take pity on her, and we will grow old together," and he added, "Amen, amen," and they went to sleep for the night.

Raguel got up, and called the house-slave to himself, and went out and dug a grave, saying, "No one must know if he has died, or I will become the object of ridicule and insults."

They finished digging the grave and Raguel returned to the house, and called his wife and said, "Send one of the young girls, and let her see whether he is alive. If he died, we can bury him and no one will know."

She sent the young girl, who lit the lamp, and opened the door, and entered, and found them lying there passed out together. The young girl left and told them they were alive and nothing evil had happened.

They praised the god Shamayim, saying, "Blessed is God in every blessing, pure and praised in everything in the ages. It has not happened, that which I suspected, but you have dealt with us according to your great mercy. Bless and take pity on the two only-children,[3] for them to be fruitful Lord. Have mercy and give them health, and bring joy and mercy to their lives."

Then he said to his house-slave, "Be cheerful and refill the grave we dug before."

The women said, "Bake a lot of bread! Go to the cattle herd and fetch two cows and four rams," and then said, "slaughter them and begin to prepare them."

He called Tobiah and said to him, "You will remain here for fourteen days, and eat and drink with me, and be cheerful with the mind of my daughter. And half of everything that I own you will receive, and return safely to your father, and the other half will be yours when I and my wife are dead. Have courage, child, I am your father and Edna is your mother, and we are your family from now for the ages, have courage child."

Tobit (Sinaiticus): Chapter 8 Notes

1) Codex Sinaiticus: ouranoe (ΟΥΡΑΝΟΙ). Translation: skies, Uranuses

The use of the Greek translation of the word Shamayim, plural for sky, combined with the reference to his house, is a clear reference to the gods Shamayim and Bethel, who are well documented in the Masoretic Texts and archaeological records as being major Israelite gods at the time that Tobiah would have been praying.

2) Codex Sinaiticus: Evan (ΕΥΑΝ)

Evan was the Greek transliteration of Eve used in the Septuagint's book of Genesis, other than the initial reference to her as Zoe (Ζωή), meaning life.

3) Codex Sinaiticus: monogenis (ΜΟΝΟΓΕΝΕΙC)

This word translates as approximately 'only member of a family,' which, strictly speaking, was not the case for Tobiah and Sarah, however, they were both the only-children of their parents, and that is likely was the Aramaic source was referring to.

Tobit (Sinaiticus): Chapter 9

Then Tobiah called Raphael, and said to him, "Azariah, brother, take with yourself four house-slaves, and two camels, and go on to Ray to visit Gabael and give him the letter, and after you have received the silver, return to the marriage. You know that my father is counting the days, and if I take even one more day, he will be very worried, however, Raguel has sworn me to stay, and I cannot leave because of the oath."

So Raphael traveled with the four house-slaves and the two camels, to Ray in Media, lodged with Gabael, and gave him the message, and told him about Tobiah, the son of Tobit, and that he took a wife, and invited him to the wedding.

And he rose counted out some seed-bags besides the amount owed and prepared everything, and they traveled together to the wedding. They entered into Raguel's and when they found Tobiah he leapt up and wept and blessed him, and said, "Noble and good man, honorable and brave, law-abiding and charitable. Lord Shamayim bless you and your wife, and the father and mother of your wife. Bless the god that saw my nephew Tobiah, who is like me."

Tobit (Sinaiticus): Chapter 10

Tobit counted day after day, and when the number of days of the journey were counted and they had not returned, then he asked, "Are they delayed, or is Gabael dead, and there is no man to give him the silver?" Then he became distressed.

Hannah his wife said, "My child is destroyed, and no longer exists, and is no longer living!" and she began to cry and sing a dirge for her son, and said, "Woe to me, children, that I sent out to walk, the light of my eyes!"

Tobit replied to her, "Calm down and think, sister. He may be safe and healthy but delayed there. The man that traveled with him is an honest brother of ours. Don't worry about him, sister. He'll return soon." He added, "Calm down, like me, and don't leap to conclusions about the death of our son, and assume without watching the road. Why grieve for our son who may return today?"

She was not convinced at all, and when the sun set sang a dirge and cry the whole night without sleeping.

When the fourteen days of the wedding had concluded, which Raguel had hosted for his daughter, Tobiah went to him and said, "I must leave. I know that my father and mother expect to see me soon. Now, I must be claiming that which my father sent me for, and must prepare to return to my family, as my father is expecting me."

Raguel replied, "Wait, child, stay with me, and I will send a messenger to Tobit your father and inform him about you."

He replied to him, "I cannot, I ask that you send me back from here to my father."

So Raguel handed over to Tobiah, Sarah his wife, and half of everything that he had, including the boy-slaves, girl-slaves, cattle, sheep, donkeys, camels, clothing, silver, and utensils. He sent them away, and sanctified them, and blessed him, saying, "Be safe, child, lead them safely. The god Shamayim will help you on the way, and Sarah your wife, and I will see your children before I die."

He said to Sarah his daughter, "Honor your parents-in-law, who are your parents now, and remain peaceful, daughter, so I may hear good things of you while I live," and bid them farewell.

Tobit (Sinaiticus): Chapter 11

When they arrived in Caserin,[1] which is near Nineveh, Raphael said, "You know, brother, how you left your father. Let's hurry ahead of your wife, and prepare the house," and so they both went ahead. He also said, "Bring the bile in your hand."

So they went their way, along with the dog.

Hannah was sitting looking down the road for her son, and when she saw him coming, she said to his father, "Look, your son comes, along with the man that went with him!"

Then Raphael said to Tobiah before they approached his father, "Know that he will open his eyes. Anoint his eyes with the bile of the fish, and they will become itchy and he will rub them, and the whiteness will fall away, and he will see you, and your father will again see the light!"

Then Hannah ran out, and fell on the neck of her son, and said to him, "Now that I have seen you, my son, I am content to die from now on!"

They both wept together. Tobit rose and put down his drink and went out the door into his courtyard, and stumbled. Tobias ran to him, and placed the bile of the fish in his eyes, and blew on the eyes, then lifted him and said, "Have courage father," and gave him the extra medicine, and pealed off the scabs from each of his eyelids with his hand.

He hugged him, and wept, and said to him, "I can see, child, with the light of my eyes!" He continued, "Bless God, and blessed his great name forever! Praise all his messengers and saints, and Amen, his great name.² Bless all the angels above us, in all their times, who he chastises with! I see Tobiah, my son!"

And so Tobit welcomed them with celebration, and blessed God for the restoration of his eyes, and Tobiah told his father of his success on the road. That he had recovered the silver, and that he had married Sarah, the daughter of Raguel's wife, and that she was approaching the gate to Nineveh.

Then Tobit went out to meet his daughter-in-law at the gate of Nineveh, rejoicing and praising God,

and those that saw him in Nineveh walking, and possessing all his faculties and without being led by the hand, marveled, and Tobit told those who approached him that God had pity on him and opened his eyes.

When he met Sarah the wife of Tobiah his son, he said to her, "Enter and be healthy, daughter, blessed is the god that led you to us, daughter, and blessed is your father, and blessed is Tobiah my son, and be celebrated, daughter. Enter your house in safety, celebration, and joy, enter, daughter."

It was a day of great joy for all the Judahites in Nineveh. Ahikar[3] and Nadan[4] his nephew came to celebrate the wedding of Tobiah.

Tobit (Sinaiticus): Chapter 11 Notes

1) Codex Sinaiticus: Caserin (ΚΑϹΕΡΕΙΝ)

- Codex Monacensis (VL 130): Cara

- Codex Sangermanensis 4 (VL 7): Caracha

- Codex Complutensis 1 (VL 109): Tarram

This town is unknown to modern archaeologists, however, is likely a Greek transliteration of the Aramaic name Kashisim (כשׁישׁ), itself a transliteration of the town called Kiššaššu (𒅅𒀸𒋢) in Assyrian. These names are mentioned in tablets found in Nineveh dating to the 7th-century BC, however, the location of the town is unknown. Given how little is known for certain about the town, a transliteration of the Greek name is used in this translation.

2) Codex Sinaiticus: Genoeto to anoma to mega autou (ΓΕΝΟΙΤΟ ΤΟ ΟΝΟΜΑ ΤΟ ΜΕΓΑ ΑΥΤΟΥ). Translation: Genoeto the name the great his

As Genoeto (Γενοιτο) was used in the Septuagint as a translation for the word that the Masoretic Texts retains as Amen (אָמֵן), the name Amen is restored in this verse, and indicates that the Samaritans, or at least the author, viewed Amen as being the name of God. There are several other verses in the books not redacted by Simon the Zealot that show the Samaritans and Judahites were sun-worshipers before being conquered by the Assyrians and Babylonians.

In 1st Ezra, Pharaoh Necho II of Egypt claimed to have been sent by Lord the god to fight the Babylonians, however, Necho II was a sun-worshiper, suggesting that the Sun was Lord the god in Judah at the time in the view of the author. King Josiah had banned the worship of the Sun, along with the moon, and Shamayim, in favor of Yahweh, and was subsequently killed by the Pharaoh, who then occupied Judah. Jeremiah, the prophet of Yahweh, who lived through this era claimed the Judahites were worshiping the wrong god, suggesting sun-worship was restored by Necho II, and Baruch later described the Sun and then stated it was the god of the Israelites in the Septuagint's book of Baruch.

3) Codex Sinaiticus: Achicar (ⲁⲭⲉⲓⲕⲁⲣ)

- Codex Vaticanus: Achiacharos (ⲁⲭⲓⲁⲭⲁⲣⲟⲥ)

- Septuagint ms. 107: Achiachar (Ⲁⲭιⲁⲭⲁⲣ)

- Codex Corbeiensis (VL 150): Achicarus

- Codex Complutensis 1 (VL 109): Acicarus

- Codex Sangermanensis 4 (VL 7): Achiacar

- Codex Bobbiensis (VL 135): Achicharus

- Codex Monacensis (VL 130): Achiar

The Codex Sinaiticus contains a curious version of Ahikar's name in this verse, which is otherwise the same as his name in the Codex Vaticanus. It appears to be a direct transliteration of the Aramaic version of the name Åḥyqr (אחיקר), suggesting the Sinaiticus translation originally used direct translations of the Aramaic names, which were replaced with the common Greek translations at some point. In any event, the Sinaiticus version must have been translated directly from an Aramaic text in order to include a transliteration of the Aramaic version of the name, which supports the Sinaiticus version being older than the Vaticanus.

4) Codex Sinaiticus: Nabad (ⲚⲀⲃⲀⲇ)

- Codex Vaticanus: Nasbas (ⲚⲀⲥⲃⲀⲥ)

- Septuagint manuscript 71: Nabas (*Ναβασ*)

- Sahidic manuscripts: Asbas (ⲀⲥⲃⲀⲥ)

- Codex Complutensis 1 (VL 190): Nabat

- Codex Regius (VL 148): Nabal

- Codex Monacensis (VL 130): Nadab

The name of the nephew is not standardized in the manuscripts. The nephew's name used in the surviving copies of the Words of Ahikar is Nadan, which is used in this translation as the copies of the Septuagint do not agree.

Tobit (Sinaiticus): Chapter 12

They completed the marriage, and Tobit called Tobiah his son and said, "Child, see that the man who went with you is paid, and you must give him a bonus."

Tobiah said to him, "Father, how much should I pay him? It won't hurt me to give him half of everything which I have brought back with me, as he has brought me back to you in safety, and saved my wife, and brought the silver to me, and also healed you. How much should I give him?"

Then he answered Tobiah, "It is justified, child, take half of all that you have brought," and he called him and said, "Take half of everything I have as your salary when you leave, and leave in peace."

Then he called them secretly and told them, "Praise God and thank him for the things which he has done to you in the sight of all that live. It is good to praise God, and exalt his name, and honorably to declare the works of God, and so don't be slow to praise him. It is good to keep private the secret of a king, but it is honorable to reveal the works of God. Do that which is good, and no evil will touch you. Prayer is good with fasting and charity and righteousness. A little with righteousness is better than much with unrighteousness. It is better to give charitably than to save up gold, for charity delivers from death, and will purge away all sin. Those who exercise charity and righteousness will be filled with life, but they who sin are enemies to their own life. Certainly, I told you the truth, and I will take nothing from you. For I said, 'It was good to keep private the secret of a king, but that it was honorable to reveal the works of God.' Now, therefore, when you prayed, and Sarah your daughter-in-law, I brought your prayers before the glorious Lord[1] and when you buried the dead, I was also with you. When you did not delay to rise and leave your dinner to go bury the dead, your good deed was not hidden from me, but I was with you. And so, God has sent me to heal you, and your daughter-in-law Sarah. I am Raphael, one of the seven holy messengers, which go in and out before the glorious Lord."

Then they were both troubled, and fell on their faces, for they were afraid. But he said to them, "Don't be afraid, for it will be well with you. Praise God, and do not ask any favor from me. By the will of our God I came, therefore praise him forever. All these days I appeared to you, but I did not eat or drink, as you were seeing a vision. Now, give praise on the Earth to the Lord and thank God. I go up to him that sent me. Write all the things which were happened to you."

When they rose, they no longer saw him. Then they praised and sang praise to God and praised his actions and

his great name, as they'd witnessed the messenger of
God.

Tobit (Sinaiticus): Chapter 12 Notes

1) Codex Sinaiticus: doxês cyriou (ⲇⲟⲍⲏⲥⲕⲨⲣⲓⲟⲨ). Translation: glorious Lord

- Codex Vaticanus: agiou (ⲀⲄⲓⲟⲨ). Translation: saint

Tobit (Sinaiticus): Chapter 13

He continued, "Blessed is the god who lives for ages, and blessed in his kingdom. For he punishes and has mercy. He leads down to the grave and brings up again, and those he chastises and plagues, Shachar[1] leads from Hades, the lowest part of the Earth. He leads up from great loss, and none exist at all that can escape his hand. Tell of him to the nations you Israelites, for he has scattered us among them. Declare his greatness and extol him before all the living, for our Lord exists, and he is our God, and our father, and he is God of everything in their ages. He will have mercy on all of you where he scattered you among the nations."

"If you turn to him with your whole heart, and with your whole mind, and deal honestly before him, then will he return to you, and will not hide his face from you. Praise Lord Sydyk,[2] and praise the king of ages. In the land of my captivity, I praise him and declare his might and majesty to a sinful nation. You sinners, turn and do justice before him. Who can tell if he will accept you, and have mercy on you?"

"I will extol my God, and my mind will praise the king of the sky, and will rejoice in his greatness, and let the streets of Jerusalem sing of joyous love, and all of her temples sing, 'Hallelujah, praise God of Israel,' and bless and praise the holy name, in the ages and now! Once more, your tabernacle will have a temple built in joy, and celebrate you, and all taken captive will be greeted with affection by you, and all their discomfort and all their generations of ages."

"Bright light shines all the way to the edge of the earth. Nations from far off depend on you and all who live to the extremities of the Earth, and call you holy, and your gifts your hands hold, King of the sky.[3] Generation after generation is always going to give you joyful praise, and chose your name in all generations of ages."

"All accursed, love difficult words. Accursed is everyone who insults you, and pulls down your walls, and knocks down your towers, burns your temples, and blessed is everyone for the ages who fear you. At that time, they will go and rejoice greatly, those sons of the law. Everyone who collects and brings to, and praises the Lord of the ages, blesses and shows affection for the dead in your peace, and blesses all people you grieve and all you scourge, and you rejoice in that you will be able to see all your joy for the ages! My mind blesses the Lord, the Great King!"[4]

"Jerusalem will be rebuilt,[5] the city of his temple in all centuries is blessed. Those born from the remnants of the descendants will see your glory and praise the king of the sky. The streets of Jerusalem will be paved in sapphires and emeralds, and all the walls will be rebuilt of precious stones. The towers of Jerusalem will be rebuilt of gold, and the bastion from pure gold, and the streets of carbuncle, with beautiful gemstones from Sauvira.[6]

The streets of Jerusalem will sing joyously and cheer-fully, and all her temples will sing, 'Hallelujah, blessed is the god of Israel, and blessed is the holy name for ages and now!'"

Tobit (Sinaiticus): Chapter 13 Notes

1) Codex Sinaiticus: eôs (ЄѠϹ). Translation Eos (or dawn)

The Titan Eos, was the Greek goddess of the dawn, whose Canaanite equivalent was Shachar (שַׁחַר), who was referred to in the book of Isaiah as the father of the morning star, later translated by Jerome as Lucifer in the Latin Vulgate. Shachar was the god of the dawn in the ancient Ugaritic Texts, however, was still worshiped as later as the time of Isaiah, who lived at approximately the same time as Tobit, therefore, the Canaanite/early-Israelite name is restored as Tobit would not have been referencing a Greek Titan.

2) Codex Sinaiticus: ton cyrion tês dicaeosynês (ΤΟΝΚΥΡΙΟΝ ΤΗϹΔΙΚΑΙΟϹΥΝΗϹ). Translation: the lord the justice

• Septuagint manuscript 249: ton theon tês dicaeosynês (τον θεον της δικαιοσυνης). Translation: the god the justice

• Codex Corbeiensis (VL 150): de dominus in iustitia. Translation: the lord in (or under, towards) Justinia

• Codex Bobbiensis (VL 135): de deum de iustitiam. Translation: the god the justice

The term 'the justice' (τῆσ Δικαιοσύνης) was used in the Septuagint for places where the Masoretic Texts retains the name Sydyk (צֶדֶק), the Canaanite god of justice. During the Roman era, the same name was applied to the Roman god Jupiter (Jove) as well as for the Roman spirit of Justice (Justitia) by Hebrew-speaking people, meaning the knowledge of Sydyk had not disappeared by the early Christian era.

3) Codex Sinaiticus: basili tou ouranou (ΒΑϹΙΛΕΙΤΟΥΟΥΡΑΝΟΥ). Translation: king the vaulted-sky (or Uranus)

• Codex Complutensis 1 (VL109): regem de caelum. Translation: king of the sky

• Codex Bobbiensis (VL 135): rex de caelum et terrae. Translation: king of the sky and land

The vaulted-sky (Οὐρανοῦ) of early Greek cosmology was based on, or very similar to, the Shamayim of the ancient Canaanite and Israelite religions, however, the term 'king' is more problematic, as the Aramaic word mlch (𐤌𐤋𐤊) is likely the source of the Septuagint's word Moloch, the name of one of the gods that Solomon set up an idol to in his temple.

The god in question was the Ammanite god mlk (𐤌𐤋𐤊), whose name translates as king, however, the god's name is not pronounced in Hebrew as melech (מֶלֶךְ), meaning king, but preserves the Aramaic spelling as mwlch (מוֹלֵךְ). This verse implies that Moloch was a title for Shamayim and Bethel, who certainly was a god being worshiped in the Temple in Jerusalem before King Josiah's reforms circa 625 BC, several decades after this book was apparently written.

4) Codex Sinaiticus: ton cyrion ton basilea ton megan (ΤΟΝ ΚΥΡΙΟΝ ΤΟΝ ΒΑϹΙΛΕΑ ΤΟΝ ΜΕΓΑΝ). Translation: the lord the king the great

• Codex Vaticanus: ton theon ton basilea ton megan (ΤΟΝ ΘΕΟΝΤΟΝΒΑϹΙΛΕΑΤΟΝΜΕΓΑΝ). Translation: the god the king the great

• Septuagint ms. 58: ton theon ton basilea ton mega (τον Θεον τον βασιλεα τον μεγα). Translation: the god the king the great

Given the pronunciation of 'king' in Aramaic, this may have read 'the god Moloch the great,' however, that cannot be proven with the surviving texts, and so a more generalized translation is used.

5) As Tobit was reported to have died before King Cyaxares (Αχιαχαρος) of Media conquered Nineveh in 612 BC, and Jerusalem wasn't destroyed by the Neo-Babylonian Empire until 587 BC, Tobit could not have predicted the rebuilding of the city that had not been destroyed yet. Another Tobit may have made the prediction. On of the original Israelite leader who returned to Jerusalem in the book of Ezra was known as Tobit, however, he was later rejected as his lineage could not be proven. Followers of a priesthood of Tobit were later reported to be active in Moab during the Persian and Greek eras, which were most likely those who used the book of Tobit.

6) Codex Vaticanus: Souphir (ⲥⲟⲩⲫⲓⲣ)

• Codex Sinaiticus: Souphir (ⲥⲟⲩⲫⲉⲓⲣ)

• Septuagint manuscript 46: Ophir (Οφειρ)

• Septuagint manuscript 583: Saphir (Σαφιρ)

• Septuagint manuscript 319: Souphêrô (Σουφηρω)

• Septuagint manuscript 107: Souphêrô (Σουφηρ)

This quasi-mythical land of riches was also transliterated as Sophira (Σωφηρα) in other books of the Septuagint, and as Ofir (אוֹפִיר) in the Masoretic Texts.

The location of this civilization has been a matter of debate for ages. Given the list of items imported from Souphir/Sophira/Ôpîr, it was likely the ancient Pakistani Kingdom of Sauvira on the Indus River. Imported items include gold, silver, sandalwood, pearls, ivory, apes, and peacocks. Sandalwood trees are indigenous to South and Southeast Asia and have traditionally been considered sacred by the Hindus, Jainists, Buddhists, and Zoroastrians, as well as other Asian cultures. Peacocks are indigenous to South and Southeast Asia, as well as the Congo Rain-forest, however, Sandalwood trees are not found in the Congo Rain-forest. Apes were still living in South and Southeast Asia circa 1000 BC, along with most of Africa.

An alternate theory regarding the location of Sophira was that it was a trading port in Southern Arabia or Somalia, however, the ships of Solomon were said to take three years to travel between Edom and Souphir/Sophira/Ofir, which makes the location of Sauvira more likely. The Kingdom of Sauvira is listed in the ancient Late Vedic period and early Buddhist literature, as well as the Mahabharata, based around its capital of Rohri in the modern Pakistani state of Sindh.

This civilization is recorded as having existed from the Early Vedic period, before 1100 BC, meaning it would have existed in the time of Solomon. The capital of Sauvira was Aror, also called Roruka or Rorik in classical literature, which was one of the most important cities in South Asia in the 7th-century BC, when this book was set. According to the Buddhist Bhallatiya Jataka, as well as Jain Story of Udayan and the town of Vitabhaya, the city of Aror was destroyed by a major sandstorm around 450 BC, following which the modern city of Rorhi (روبـژى / روهـژي) was founded around 10 kilometers away.

Tobit (Sinaiticus): Chapter 14

Here end the words of the statement of Tobit.

He died peacefully at 112 years old, and was buried honorably in Nineveh. He had been 62 years old when he became blind, and after becoming blind lived morally on charity donated to him, and yet put God first and praised the greatness of God.

When he was dying, he called Tobiah his son, and said, "Child, take your children, and move to Media, as I believe the declaration of God against Nineveh spoken by Nahum,[1] the everything that exists in Assur[2] and Nineveh, and as the prophet of Israel said, who was sent by God, 'All happened, and never did even one small word not happen, always it happened according to his time.' In Media exists salvation rather than in Assyria or in Babylon. Because I know and have faith whatever God said always takes place and happens, and not even a word fails from his message."

"Our brothers, the residents in the land of Israel, and everyone dispersed and taken captive from the land, and the goods, that exists in all the desolate land of Israel and the Samaria and Jerusalem are desolate and the temple of God is afflicted and set on fire for all time. Again God will have mercy on them, and God will return them to the land of Israel, and the temple will be rebuilt, not like the first at the dawn of time. It will be completed at the specified time, and with those returned from the captives, each and every one, who will rebuild Jerusalem and the Temple of God, and rebuild every-thing, as stated by the prophets of Israel."

"All the nations of the whole Earth, every one will turn and will genuinely fear God. Abandon all their idols, and those who cause to wander through cheating by lying about the planets, and praise the Lord for the ages in justice.

"All sons of Israel, those saved in all the days, who recall God in truth, and are collected and brought to Jerusalem and inhabit the land of Abraham in security, and safety for the ages. Rejoice and truly show affection for God, and abandon the errors and injustices of all kinds on the Earth."

"Now, child, I say to you, you worked for God in truth and you sang that which is acceptable in front of him. The children you made captives to bring justice and charity, and so they would remember God and praise his name for all time in truth and with their entire might."

"Now you, child, leave Nineveh and don't delay here. On the day you bury your mother with me, on that day, don't remain on this side of the border. Look around at all the injustice, and great deceit to gain through any means with no shame!"

"Remember, child, how Nadan treated Ahikar who raised him, not to live, but to be taken down into the earth? Yet God banished the dishonor against him and Ahikar came out into the light, and Nadan entered into the darkness for the ages for seeking to kill Ahikar. He gave charitably and escaped the snares of death which they had set for him, but Nadan fell into the snare and perished. Now, child, see what charity does, and what injustice brings?"

"My mind is leaving..."

They left him on the bed, and he died, and they buried him honorably.

They held an honorable feast in Ecbatana in Media, and invited the house of Raguel from Tobit's father.

He died at 117 years old in high esteem, however, saw and heard before he died, of the fall of Nineveh, and how she was captured and ruled by Media, and had been taken prisoner by King Cyaxares[3] of Media. He praised the God of everything, that he brought this on Nineveh and the Assyrians. He was cheerful that this happened to Nineveh before he died, and praised the Lord of ages and ages.

Tobit (Sinaiticus): Chapter 14 Notes

1) Codex Sinaiticus: Naoum (ναογμ)

• Codex Vaticanus: Iônas (ιωναϲ)

Both Nahum and Jonah predicted the destruction of Nineveh. The Book of Nahum is internally dated sometime during and shortly after the Assyrian occupation of Egypt between 663 and 656 BC, and generally accepted as dating to that era, while Jonah is widely regarded as being fiction by historians.

The Book of Jonah is internally dated sometime during the Assyrian rule of Samaria, approximately 720 to 612 BC. If Jonah and Tobit were both real people, they would have been in Nineveh at the same time, and given the size of the Samaritan population in Nineveh, likely would have met.

2) Codex Sinaiticus: Athêr (ΑΘΗΡ)

• Codex Corbeiensis (VL 150): Assur

• Codex Monacensis (VL 130): Assyr

• Codex Bobbiensis (VL 135): Assyrios

Based on the contexts, it is clear that Assur, the capital of Assyria is intended, however, the Codex Sinaiticus' transliteration of the name appears to be based on the Persian version of the name: Athur (𐎰𐎢𐎼), suggesting the Aramaic translation was made in Persia or Media.

3) Codex Sinaiticus: Achiacharos (ΑΧΕΙΑΧΑΡΟϹ)

• Codex Vaticanus: Nabouchodonosor cae Asyêros (ΝΑΒΟΥΧΟΔΟΝΟϹΟΡ ΚΑΙ ΑϹΥΗΡΟϹ). Translation: Nabouchodonosor and Asyeros

• Codex Alexandrinus: Nabouchodonosor cae Asouchros (ΝΑΒΟΥΧΟΔΟΝΟϹΟΡ ΚΑΙ ΑϹΟΥΧΡΟϹ). Translation: Nabouchodonosor and Asouchros

• Septuagint ms. 319: Nabouchodonosor cae Assyêros (Ναβουχοδονοσορ και Ασσυηρος). Translation: Nabouchodonosor and Assyeros

• Septuagint ms. 46: Nabouchodonosor cae Asoêros (Ναβουχοδονοσορ και Ασοηρος). Translation: Nabouchodonosor and Asoeros

• Septuagint ms. 488: Nabouchodonosor cae Assoucros (Ναβουχοδονοσορ και Ασσουκρος). Translation: Nabouchodonosor and Assoucros

This final line appears to be part of an anachronistic redaction. The Babylonian King Nabopolassar sacked Nineveh in 612 BC, along with Median and Persian allies. His son Nebuchadnezzar, who assumed the throne in 605 BC, finally conquered the remnants of the Assyrian forces in Syria at the Battle of Carchemish that same year, however, he did not destroy Nineveh. The name Asyêros (Ασυηρος) is generally accepted as a variant spelling of Ahasuerus (Ασουηρος), the Aramaic name of Xerxes, the Persian king who ruled between 486 and 465 BC.

The Codex Sinaiticus' does not mention either king, but gives credit to King Achiacharos (Αχιαχαρος) of Media, which is likely an attempt to transliterate the name Uvaxštra (𐎢𐎺𐎧𐏁𐎫𐎼), which was also transliterated as Cyaxarês (Κυαξάρης) in Greek, from which his common English name is derived. Other ancient versions of his name include the Elamite Makiišturri (𒌋𒀖𒁹𒐊𒆠), Neo-Babylonian Úaksatar (𒌍𒐊𒐊𒐊𒊏𒀭), and the Phrygian Ksuwaksaros (ΚϹΟͰΑϒϹΡΟϹ). Cyaxares was the Median king who fought alongside the Babylonian King Nabopolassar at the sack of Nineveh, following which Nineveh became part of his Median Empire. This seems clear proof that the Codex Sinaiticus version of Tobit is older, and more accurate.

Words of Ahihar: Chapter 1

This is the story of Ahikar[1] the sage, vizier of King Sennacherib,[2] and of Ahikar's nephew Nadan.[3]

There was a vizier in the days of King Sennacherib, son of King Esarhaddon[4] of Nineveh in Assyria, a wise man named Ahikar. He had a great fortune and a great deal of property, and he was skillful, wise, a philosopher in knowledge, and opinionated in government. He had married sixty women and had built a mansion for each of them. Yet he had no child by any of these women who could be his heir. He was very sad on account of this, and one day he assembled the astrologers and the learned men and the wizards and explained to them his condition and the matter of his barrenness. They said to him, "Go, sacrifice to the gods and beg them, maybe they will provide you with a son."

He did as they told him and offered sacrifices to the idols, and prayed to them and begged them with requests. They did not answer him even one word. He went away sad and dejected, departing with a pain at his heart. He returned and implored the Highest God,[5] and believed, begging him with a burning in his heart, saying, "Highest God, creator of the skies and the earth, creator of all created things! I beg you to give me a son, that I may be consoled by him, and that he may be present in my home, and that he may close my eyes, and that he may bury me."

Then there came to him a voice saying, "As you have relied first of all on carved statues, and have offered sacrifices to them, for this reason, you will remain childless your whole life. But adopt Nadan your sister's son, and make him your child and teach him what you've learned and your good breeding, and at your death, he will bury you."

Thereafter he took Nadan his sister's son, who was still an infant. He handed him over to eight wet-nurses, that they might suckle him and raise him. They raised him with good food and gentle training and silk clothing, and purple and crimson, and he was seated on couches of silk. When Nadan grew big and walked, shooting up like a tall cedar, he taught him good manners and writing and science and philosophy.

After many days King Sennacherib looked at Ahikar and saw that he had grown very old, and he said to him, "My honored friend, the skillful, trustworthy, wise governor, my secretary, my vizier, my chancellor, and director. You have grown very old and weighted with years, and your departure from this world must be near. Tell me who will have a place in my service after you."

Ahikar said to him, "My lord, may you live forever! There is Nadan my sister's son, I have adopted him as my child. I have brought him up and taught him my wisdom and knowledge."

The king said to him, "Ahikar, bring him into my presence so I may see him, and if I find him suitable put him in your place, and you will go your way, to take a rest and to live the remainder of your life in sweet repose."

Then Ahikar went and presented Nadan his sister's son. He paid homage and wished him power and honor. He looked at him and admired him and rejoiced in him and said to Ahikar, "Is this your son, Ahikar? I pray that God may preserve him. As you have served me and my father Esarhaddon so may this boy of your serve me and fulfill my desires, needs, and business, so that I may honor him and make him powerful for your sake."

Ahikar paid obeisance to the king and said to him, "May you live forever, my lord king! I ask you that you may be patient with my boy Nadan and forgive his mistakes, so he may serve you as it is fitting."

Then the king swore to him that he would make him the greatest of his favorites, and the most powerful of his friends and that he should be with him in all honor and respect. He kissed his hands and bid him farewell. He took Nadan, his sister's son with him and seated him in a parlor and set about teaching him night and day until he had filled him with wisdom and knowledge more than with bread and water.

Words of Ahihar: Chapter 1 Notes

1) Aramaic: Åḥyqr (קﬧﬡﬣﬡ)

* Greek: Achiacharos (Αχιαχαρος)

* Armenian Xikar (Խիկար)

* Arabic: Ḥayqār (حَيْقَار)

* Old Slavonic: Akyrios (Ⰰⰽⱏⱃⰻⱁⱄ)

The variations of the name Ahikar transliterated into various translations of the book indicate that most copies were made from the Aramaic version of the book. The Codex Sinaiticus' Tobit, chapter 11 also includes a direct translation of the Aramaic name as Achicar (Αχικαρ), confirming that the Aramaic translation of Tobit used the same name for him.

2) Aramaic: Snḥryb (ﬡﬦﬣﬠﬢﬤ)

* Greek: Sanacharibos (Σαναχάριβος)

* Armenian: Sinak'erib (Սինաքերիբ)

* Arabic: Snḥāryb (سنحاريب)

King Sîn-aḥḥī-erība (𒁹𒀭𒌍𒉽𒋀) was the king of the Assyrian Empire between 705 and 681 BC. While all surviving versions of the Words of Ahikar agree that it was Sennacherib, the actual successor to Esarhaddon was Ashurbanipal, indicating that the name of Ashurbanipal was redacted. The oldest copy of the book, an Aramaic copy that had been in use at the Israelite Temple of Elephantine used the name Bel where the later translations substituted 'God' or 'Lord,' indicating that the Aramaic translation was created in the Neo-Babylonian Empire, explaining why Ashurbanipal's name was removed from the text. Ashurbanipal

162

devastated Babylonia and Elam during the civil/international war against his brother Shamash-shum-ukin and his allies in Elam in the 640s BC. The Assyrians won the war, but at such a tremendous financial cost, and with such a loss of prestige, that Nabopolassar was able to lead another Babylonian revolt in the 620s BC, a few years after Ashurbanipal's death. This rebellion drew in virtually all of Assyria's neighbors, and ultimately destroyed the Neo-Assyrian Empire, dividing its territory between the newly independent Neo-Babylonian Empire, Median Empire, Kingdom of Persia, and Scythian Confederation. When the Aramaic version of Ahikar was translated, Ashurbanipal would have been seen in a similar light to how Hitler was viewed after the Second World War, making his redaction from the text a necessity.

Additionally, Ahikar could not have worked for Sennacherib, who was one of the Assyrian Kings that conquered his homeland of Samaria and exiled his people. Sennacherib would not have sent a Samaritan captive to represent him in negotiations in Egypt or Elam. The Book of Tobit recorded that both Tobit and Ahikar worked for Esarhaddon, however, Ahikar was Tobit's nephew, and therefore would have continued to work for Esarhaddon's successor Ashurbanipal. Unfortunately, all known copies of Ahikar are based on the Aramaic translation, and therefore include this anachronism.

3) Aramaic: Ndn (𐤍𐤃𐤍)

- Greek: Nadab (Ναβαδ)

- Armenian: Nadin (Նադիհու)

- Arabic: Nbāb (نباب)

Nadan's name is not standardized, and appears to have diverged during the Persian era. This translation uses the Aramaic variant of Ndn, which is probably the original, and certainly served as the source for the Armenian variant of Nadin. The Greek of Nabab and

Arabic variant of Nbāb, probably reflect a Persian era Moabite reinterpretation within the Aramaic versions of Ahikar. Ndb (𐤍𐤃𐤁) was a Moabite word meaning 'willing,' and often used in religious context for one who is 'willing to serve a god,' such as the name Chemosh-nadab (𐤊𐤌𐤔𐤍𐤃𐤁), a Moabite king who agreed to pay tribute to Assyria after Sennacherib's Levantine Wars.

4) Aramaic: Åsrḥdwn (𐤀𐤔𐤓𐤇𐤃𐤍)

* Greek: Esarhaddon (Εσαρχαδδών)

* Arabic: Åsrḥdwn (آسرحدون)

Aššur-aḫa-iddina, more commonly known as Esarhaddon from the Hebrew version of his name Ēsar-ḥaddōn (אֵסַר־חַדֹּן) was actually Sennacherib's son, not his father. Esarhaddon was the king of the Assyrian Empire between 681 and 669 BC. He is famous for conquering Egypt and creating the largest Empire in Middle-eastern history until then.

5) The Highest is a reference to God, or a god, found in many ancient religions in the region. According to the Torah, the ancient people of Jerusalem worshiped El elyovn (אֵל עֶלְיוֹן), which translates as 'God highest' when Abraham passed through the region. The Greeks translated it as theô tô ypsistô (Θεω τω υψιστω) in the Septuagint, also meaning 'God the highest.' El elyovn is known to have been a major god of the Canaanites, called ål wålyn (𐤀𐤋 𐤅𐤏𐤋𐤉𐤍), meaning 'God and highest' in an Aramaic language Sefire Treaty from circa 750 BC.

The Greek translations of Sanchuniathon's bronze age writing that have survived to the present, referred to the primordial creator god of the Canaanites as Elioun (Ελιουν), which appears to be the same god. According to Sanchuniathon, Elioun was the 'highest' (υψιστος) god, who made the sky and the land, and they made the rest of the gods. While the many references to Bel in this text appear to refer to the Babylonian god Bel, these references to the Highest are clearly references to the old Canaanite god El elyovn. A version of El elyovn was worshiped by the Neo-Assyrians in the form of ^{deity}Šar (𒀭𒊹), more commonly called Anshar today. Anshar translates directly as 'deity totality' or 'deity eternity,' and was perceived in the later Neo-Assyrian era as the patriarch of the gods who created everything.

Words of Ahihar: Chapter 2

He taught him, saying, "My son! Hear my speech and follow my advice and remember what I say.

My son, if you hear a word, let it remain in your heart, and don't reveal it to another, in case it becomes a lump of burning coal and burns your tongue and causes pain in your body, and you become reproachful and are shamed before God and man.

My son, if you have heard a report, don't spread it, and if you have seen something, don't tell it.

My son, make your speech easy to the listener and do not rush to answer questions.

My son, when you have heard anything, don't hide it.

My son, don't loosen a sealed knot, or untie it, and don't seal a loosened knot.

My son, don't covet outward beauty, for it fades and passes away, but instead an honorable memory that lasts forever.

My son, don't let a foolish woman deceive you with her speech, in case you die the most miserable of deaths, and she entangles you in a net until you are trapped.

My son, don't desire a woman beautified with clothing and with ointments, who is despicable and foolish in her mind. Woe to you if you bestow on her anything that is yours or commit to her what is in your hand and she entices you into sin, and God becomes angry with you.

My son, do not be like the almond-tree, for it brings out leaves before all the trees, and edible fruit after them all, but be like the mulberry-tree, which brings out edible fruit before all the trees, and leaves after them all.

My son, bend your head low down, and soften your voice, and be courteous, and walk in the straight path, and don't be foolish. Don't raise your voice when you laugh for if it were by a loud voice that a house was built, the donkey would build many houses every day, and if it were just through strength that the plow was driven, the plow would never be removed from under the shoulders of the camels.

My son, the moving of stones with a wise man is better than the drinking of wine with a foolish man.

My son, pour out your wine on the tombs of the just and don't drink with ignorant, contemptible people.

My son, cling to wise men who fear God and be like them, and don't go near the ignorant, in case you become like him and learn his ways.

My son, when you have a comrade or a friend, test him, and afterward make him a comrade and a friend, and do not praise him without testing him. Do not waste your speech with a man who lacks wisdom.

My son, while a shoe stays on your foot, walk with it on the thorns, and make a road for your son, and for your household and your children, and make your ship taut before she goes on the sea and its waves and sinks and cannot be saved.

My son, if the rich man eats a snake, they say, "It is through his wisdom," and if a poor man eats it, the people say, "Because he is hungry."

My son, be content with your daily bread and your goods and don't covet what is another's.

My son, don't be neighbor to the fool, and don't eat bread with him, and don't rejoice in the calamities of your neighbors. If your enemy wrongs you, show him kindness.

My son, a man who fears God, fears him and honors him.

My son, the ignorant man falls and stumbles, and the wise man, even if he stumbles is not shaken, and even if he falls, he gets up quickly, and if he is sick he can take care of his life. But as for the ignorant, stupid man, there is no drug for his disease.

My son, if a man approaches you who is inferior to yourself, go forward to meet him and remain on your feet. If he cannot repay you, his lord will repay you for him.

My son, don't spare beating your son, for the beating of your son is like manure to the garden, and like tying the opening of a purse, and like the tethering of beasts, and like the bolting of the door.

My son, restrain your son from wickedness, and teach him manners before he rebels against you and brings you into contempt among the people and you hang your head in the streets and the assemblies and you be punished for the evil of his wicked deeds.

My son, get a fat ox with a foreskin, and a donkey with great hoofs, and don't get an ox with large horns, or make friends with a deceitful man, or get a quarrelsome slave, or a thievish handmaid, for everything which you give to them they will ruin.

My son, don't let your parents curse you, and the Lord[1] be pleased with them, for it has been said, "He who despises his father or his mother, let him die the death and he who honors his parents will prolong his days and his life and will see all that is good."

My son, don't travel the road without weapons, for you don't know when a foe may meet you, and you should be ready for him.

My son, do not be like a bare, leafless tree that does not grow, but be like a tree covered with its leaves and its boughs, for the man who has neither wife nor children is disgraced in the world and is hated by them, like a leafless and fruitless tree.

My son, be like a fruitful tree on the roadside, whose fruit is eaten by all who pass by, and the beasts of the desert rest under its shade and eat of its leaves.

My son, every sheep that wanders from its path and its companions becomes food for the wolf.

My son, don't say, "My lord is a fool and I am wise," and don't relate the speech of ignorance and folly, in case you become hated by him.

My son, don't be one of those servants, to who their lords say, "Get away from us," but be one of those to whom they say, "Approach and come near to us."

My son, don't caress your slave in the presence of his companion, for you don't know which of them will be of most value to you in the end.

My son, don't be afraid of the Lord who created you, in case he is silent to you.

My son, make your speech fair and sweeten your tongue, and don't let your companion step on your foot, in case at another time he steps on your chest.

My son, if you defeat a wise man with a word of wisdom, it will lurk in his chest like a subtle sense of shame, but if you beat the ignorant with a stick he will neither understand nor hear.

My son, if you send a wise man for your needs, do not give him many orders, for he will do your business as you desire, and if you send a fool, do not order him, but go yourself and do your business, for if you order him, he will not do what you desire. If they send you on business, hurry to fulfill it quickly.

My son, don't make an enemy of a man stronger than yourself, for he will take your measure, and his revenge on you.

My son, test your son, and your servant, before you trust your belongings to them, in case they run away with them, for he who has a full hand is called wise, even if he is stupid and ignorant, and he who has an empty hand is called poor and ignorant, even if he is the prince of sages.

My son, I have eaten colocynth,[2] and swallowed bitters, and I have found nothing more bitter than poverty and scarcity.

My son, teach your son frugality and hunger, that he may do well in the management of his household.

My son, don't teach the ignorant the language of wise men, for it will be burdensome to him.

My son, don't display your condition to your friend, in case you become despised by him.

My son, the blindness of the heart is more terrible than the blindness of the eyes, for the blindness of the eyes may be guided little by little, but the blindness of the heart is not guided, and it leaves the straight path and goes in a crooked way.

My son, the stumbling of a man with his foot is better than the stumbling of a man with his tongue.

My son, a friend who is near is better than a more excellent brother who is far away.

My son, beauty fades but learning lasts, and the world fades and becomes vain, but a good name neither becomes vain nor fades.

My son, for the man who has no peace, his death is better than his life, and the sound of mourning is better than the sound of singing. If the fear of God is in them, sorrow and weeping are better than the sound of singing and rejoicing.

My child, the leg of a frog in your hand is better than a goose in the pot of your neighbor, and a sheep near you is better than an ox far away, and a sparrow in your hand is better than a thousand sparrows flying. Poverty

172

which gathers is better than the scattering of many provisions, and a living fox is better than a dead lion. A pound of wool is better than a pound of gold or silver, for the gold and the silver are hidden and covered up in the earth and are not seen, but the wool stays in the markets and it is seen, and it is a beauty to him who wears it.

My son, a small fortune is better than a scattered fortune.

My son, a living dog is better than a dead poor man.

My son, a poor man who does right is better than a rich man who is dead because of his sins.

My son, keep a word in your heart, and it will be much to you and beware that you don't reveal the secret of your friend.

My son, don't let a word issue from your mouth until you have taken counsel with your heart. Stand not between quarreling people, because from an insult there comes a quarrel, and from a quarrel there comes a dispute, and from dispute there comes fighting, and you will be forced to bear witness. Instead, run from there and have peace.

My son, don't struggle with a man stronger than yourself, but have a patient spirit, and endure in upright conduct, for there is nothing more excellent than that.

My son, don't hate your first friend, for the second one may not last.

My son, visit the poor in his affliction, and speak of him in the king's presence, and do your diligence to save him from the mouth of the lion.

My son, don't rejoice in the death of your enemy, for after a little while you will be his neighbor, and he who mocks you, you respect and honor and greeting him first.

My son, if water would stand still in the sky, and a black crow become white, and myrrh grows sweet as honey, then ignorant men and fools might understand and become wise.

My son, if you desire to be wise, restrain your tongue from lying, and your hand from stealing, and your eyes from seeing evil, and then you will be called wise.

My son, let the wise man beat you with a wand but don't let the fool anoint you with sweet salve. Be humble in your youth and you will be honored in your old age.

My son, don't stand against a man in the days of his power, or a river in the days of its flood.

My son, do not rush to wed a wife, for if it turns out well, she will say, "My lord, make provision for me," and if it turns out poorly, she will accuse him who was the cause of it.

My son, whoever is elegant in his dress, he is the same in his speech, and he who has a mean appearance in his dress, he also is the same in his speech.

My son, if you have committed a theft, make it known to the king, and give him a share of it, that you may be delivered from him, for otherwise, you will endure bitterness.

My son, make a friend of the man whose hand is satisfied and filled and don't make friends with the man whose hand is closed and hungry.

There are four things in which neither the king nor his army can be secure: oppression by the vizier, bad government, perversion of the will, and tyranny over the subjects, and four things which cannot be hidden: the prudent, the foolish, the rich, and the poor."

Words of Ahihar: Chapter 2 Notes

1) Aramaic: Bôlâ (ꓨᒪᔨᏚ). Translation: Bel (or Ba'al, Lord)

• Greek: Cyrios (Κύριος). Translation: lord

• Armenian: Ter (ՏԲր). Translation: owner (or lord, master)

• Arabic: āllh (الله). Translation: god

• Old Slavonic: Gospodĭ (ⰳⱁⱄⱂⱁⰴⰹ). Translation: lord (or master)

The various later translations indicate that the Christian and/or Islamic God is being referred to, however, scholars believe the Aramaic version was referring to Bel, the supreme god of the Neo-Babylonian pantheon. If this analysis is correct, it means the Neo-Assyrian Cuneiform text of Ahikar must have been translated into Aramaic in the Neo-Babylonian Empire, which supports the removal of the name of Ashurbanipal. Bel was worshiped by the Babylonians in the first millennium BC. He was a syncretization of the older Mesopotamian Marduk, Enlil, and Dumuzid. However, his name simply translates as 'Lord,' meaning that Ahikar could have simply been using the term 'Lord.'

Whichever god Ahikar was referring to, if he was living in Assyria under Ashurbanipal, he would not have been worshiping the god of the renegade Neo-Babylonians, meaning that Bel can only be accepted as the original god in the text if it is assumed that Ahikar did not exist, and the book is a work of fiction, written in the Neo-Babylonian era. However, this also seems improbable, as a book about a Samaritan worshiper of Bel living in the Neo-Assyrian Empire, should anyone decide to write something so obscure, would have been written in Neo-Babylonian Cuneiform, and probably not translated into Aramaic until the Persian era, resulting in the reading of 'Bel' being erased by the Israelites abandoning the title Ba'al for their god during the Neo-Babylonian era in response

Bel being the supreme god of the people who destroyed Jerusalem. As the setting of the book is Assyria, not Babylonia, the Assyrian reading of Belu (-𒂗) is used in this translation, generally rendering the term as 'Lord,' as it appears in Greek, Aramaic, and Old Slavonic translations.

There are specific references to an Idol of Bel/Lord/Allah, however, as there was no known statue at the time of the Lord or Allah, the translation of Bel is used, however, it is unlikely Bel was originally in the Neo-Assyrian text. The references to the Idol of Bel, take place in 'Egypt,' which may have been Kush at the time when Ahikar was speaking to the Pharaoh, indicating that the author was referring to an Egyptian or Kushite god, not a Babylonian god. As the name of the god is no longer in any of the texts, the reference to Bel is used in relation to the idol.

2) Colocynth, also called bitter apples, is a viny plant native to the Mediterranean region and was once cultivated across Anatolia, the Middle East, Egypt, and Kush. It was cultivated in Egypt since pre-Dynastic times, since at least 3800 BC. By the classical era, it was mainly used for medicine. Today it is primarily cultivated for medicine or bio-fuel.

Words of Ahihar: Chapter 3

So spoke Ahikar, and when he had finished these injunctions and proverbs to Nadan, his sister's son, he imagined that he would keep them all, and he did not know that instead, that he was seeing him as weary and contemptible, and mocking him. Ahikar sat in his house afterward and gave to Nadan all his goods, and the slaves, and the handmaidens, and the horses, and the livestock, and everything else that he had possessed and gained, and the power of bidding and of forbidding was given to the hand of Nadan. Ahikar sat in peace in his house, and occasionally Ahikar went and paid his respects to the king, and returned home.

When Nadan saw that the power of bidding and forbidding was in his hands, he despised the position of Ahikar and scoffed at him, and set about blaming him whenever he appeared, saying, "My uncle Ahikar is in his old age, and he knows nothing anymore."

He began to beat the slaves and the handmaidens and to sell the horses and the camels and he spent all that his uncle Ahikar had owned. When Ahikar saw that he had no compassion on his servants or his household, he arose and chased him from his house, and sent a message to inform the king that he had scattered his possessions and his provision.

The king arose and called Nadan and said to him, "While Ahikar remains in health, no one will rule his goods, or his household, or over his possessions."

The hand of Nadan was lifted off from his uncle Ahikar and all his goods, and in the meantime, he neither went in or out nor did he greet him. Afterward, Ahikar regretted the struggle with Nadan his sister's son, and he continued to be very sad. Nadan had a younger brother named Benuzardan, so Ahikar took him for himself instead of Nadan, and raised him and honored him with the greatest honors. He gave over to him all that he possessed and made him ruler of his house.

Now when Nadan found out what had happened he was seized with envy and jealousy, and he began to complain to everyone who questioned him, and to mock his, uncle Ahikar, saying, "My uncle has chased me from his house and has preferred my brother to me, but if the Highest God gives me the power, I will cause him to be killed."

Nadan thought about what trap he might set for him. After a while, Nadan turned it over in his mind and wrote a letter to Achish,[1] son of King Wise,[2] the king of Persia,[3] saying:

"Peace and health and strength and honor from Sennacherib, king of Nineveh in Assyria, and from his vizier and his secretary Ahikar to you, great king! Let there be peace between you and me.

When this letter reaches you, if you will rise and go quickly to the plains of the protectors,[4] and to Nineveh in Assyria, I will deliver up the kingdom to you without war and without a battle-formation."

He wrote also another letter in the name of Ahikar to Pharaoh king of Egypt:[5]

"Let there be peace between you and me, mighty king!

If at the time when this letter reaches you, you rise and go to Nineveh in Assyria to the plain of the protectors, I will deliver up to you the kingdom without war and without fighting."

The letters of Nadan looked like the letters of his uncle Ahikar. He folded the two letters and sealed them with the seal of his uncle Ahikar, and they were left in the king's palace. Then he went and wrote a similar letter from the king to his uncle Ahikar:

"Peace and health to my vizier, my secretary, my chancellor, Ahikar,

Ahikar, when this letter reaches you, assemble all the soldiers who are with you, and let them be in perfect clothing and in great numbers, and bring them to me on the fifth day in the plain of the protectors.

When you see me there coming towards you, quickly have the army move against me like an enemy who would fight with me, for I have with me the ambassadors of Pharaoh king of Egypt, that they may see the strength of our army and may fear us, for they are our enemies and they hate us."

Then he sealed the letter and sent it to Ahikar by one of the king's servants. He took the other letter which he had written and spread it before the king and read it to him and showed him the seal. When the king heard what was in the letter he was perplexed and greatly confused and fiercely angry, and said, "Oh, I have been shown wisdom! What have I done to Ahikar that he has written these letters to my enemies? Is this my repayment for my gifts to him?'

Nadan said to him, "Do not be sad, king! Nor be angry, but let us go to the plain of the protectors and see if the story is true or not."

Then Nadan arose on the fifth day and took the king and the soldiers and the vizier, and they went to the desert to the plain of the protectors. The king looked and saw Ahikar and the army set in formation. When Ahikar saw that the king was there, he approached and signaled to the army to move as they would in war and to fight in formation against the king as it had been told in the letter, not knowing the trap Nadan had set for him.

When the king saw the acts of Ahikar he was seized with anxiety and terror and confusion and was very angry. Nadan said to him, "Have you seen, my lord the king, what this wretch has done? Do not be angry and do not be sad or hurt, but go to your house and sit on your throne, and I will bring Ahikar to you bound and chained with chains, and I will chase away your enemy from before you without a battle."

The king returned to his throne, being provoked about Ahikar, and did nothing about him. Nadan went to Ahikar and said to him, "Hello, my uncle! The king is very happy with you, and thanks you for having done what he commanded you. Now he has sent me to you that you may dismiss the soldiers to their duties and come yourself to him with your hands bound behind you, and your feet chained, that the ambassadors of Pharaoh may see this and that the king may be feared by them and by their king."

Then Ahikar answered, "To hear is to obey."

He arose right away and bound his hands behind him, and chained his feet, and Nadan took him to the king. When Ahikar entered the king's presence he did obeisance before him on the ground and wished for power and perpetual life to the king. Then the king demanded, "Ahikar, my secretary, the governor of my affairs, my chancellor, the ruler of my state, tell me what evil have

I done to you that you have rewarded me by this terrible deed."

Then they showed him the letters in his writing and with his seal. When Ahikar saw this, his limbs trembled and his tongue was tied at once, and he was unable to speak a word from fear, but he hung his head towards the earth and was dumb. When the king saw this, he felt certain that the scheme was from him, and he immediately rose and commanded them to execute Ahikar and to chop his neck with the sword outside of the city. Then Nadan screamed and said, "Ahikar! What makes you thing you can do things to the king?"

(So says the story-teller.)

The name of the swordsman was Abi Samik. The king said to him, "Swordsman! Rise and go cut the neck of Ahikar at the door of his house, and throw away his head from his body a hundred cubits."

Then Ahikar knelt before the king, and said, "Let my lord the king live forever! If you desire to slay me, let your wish be fulfilled, and I know that I am not guilty, but the wicked man has to give an account of his wickedness, nevertheless, my lord the king, I beg of you and from your friendship, permit the swordsman to give my body to my slaves, that they may bury me, and let your slave be your sacrifice."

The king rose and commanded the swordsman to do with him according to his desire. He immediately commanded his servants to take Ahikar and the swordsman and take him naked, so they might slay him. When Ahikar knew for certain that he was to be slain he sent a message to his wife, and said to her, "Come out and meet me, and let there be with you a thousand young virgins, and dress them in gowns of purple and silk that they may cry for me before my death. Prepare a table for the swordsman and his servants, and prepare plenty of wine, that they may drink."

She did all that he commanded her. She was very wise, clever, and prudent. She united all possible courtesy and learning. When the army of the king and the swordsman arrived, he found the table set in order, and the wine and the luxurious viands, and they began eating and drinking till they were gorged and drunken.

Then Ahikar took the swordsman aside, separate from the company and said, "Abi Samik, do you not know that when Esarhaddon the king, the father of Sennacherib, wanted to kill you, I took you and hid you in a certain place until the king's anger subsided and he asked for you? When I brought you into his presence he rejoiced in you, and now remember the kindness I did you. I know that the king will be sorry about me and will be very angry about my execution."

"For I am not guilty, and it will happen when you present me before him in his palace, you will meet with great fortune, and know that Nadan my sister's son has deceived me and has done this terrible deed to me, and the king will repent of having killed me. I have a well in the garden of my house, and no one knows of it. Hide me in it with only my wife knowing. I have a slave in prison who deserves to be killed. Bring him out and dress him in my clothes, and command the servants when they are drunk to slay him. They will not know who it is they are killing. Throw away his head a hundred cubits from his body, and give his body to my slaves that they may bury it. You have laid up a great treasure with me."

Then the swordsman did as Ahikar had commanded him, and he went to the king and said to him, "May you live forever!"

Then each week, Ahikar's wife lowered down to him in his hiding-place everything he needed, and no one else knew of it. The story was reported and repeated and spread abroad in every place of how Ahikar the Sage had been slain and was dead, and all the people of that city mourned for him. They wept and said, "Alas for you, Ahikar, and for your learning and your courtesy! How sad it is to lose you and your knowledge! Where can another like you be found? Where can there be a man so intelligent, learned, and skilled in ruling as to resemble you that he may fill your place?"

The king repented killing Ahikar, but his repentance did not help him. Then he called for Nadan and said to him, "Go, and take your friends with you, and mourn and cry for your uncle Ahikar, and lament for him as is the custom, honoring in his memory."

But when Nadan, the foolish, the ignorant, the hard-hearted, went to the house of his uncle, he neither wept nor mourned nor wailed, but assembled heartless and dissolute people and set about eating and drinking. Nadan began to seize the woman-slaves and the men-slaves belonging to Ahikar, and bound them and tortured them and beat them severely. He did not respect the wife of his uncle, she who had brought him up like her own son, but wanted her to sin with him. Ahikar had been in the hiding-place, and he heard the weeping of his slaves and his neighbors, and he praised the Highest God, the Merciful One, and gave thanks, and he continued to pray and implore the Highest God.

The swordsman came from time to time to Ahikar while he was in the hiding-place, and Ahikar came and begged him. He comforted him and wished him deliverance. When the story was reported in other countries that Ahikar the Sage had been murdered, all the kings were sad and hated king Sennacherib, and they lamented over Ahikar the solver of riddles.

Words of Ahihar: Chapter 3 Notes

1) Aramaic: Åkiš (𐤏𐤊𐤉𐤔)

- Greek: Acchous (Ακχους)
- Armenian: Akhis (Ախիհu)
- Arabic: Åẖyš (أخيش)

While the text refers to this as the son of 'King Wise of Persia,' it is likely that this began as a reference the Aramean chieftain Bel-Iqisha, who led an Elamite backed rebellion in southern Babylonian in 665 BC. Åkiš (𐤀𐤊𐤉𐤔) was also a popular Canaanite name at the time, and several Philistine kings bore the name, which was recorded in Neo-Assyrian Cuneiform as Ikaúsu (𒄿𒅗𒌑𒋢).

2) All translations refer to a 'King Wise, however, there are no records of any Persian king named any variation of the word 'wise,' and at Persia did not exist as a kingdom at the time, this was probably a mistranslation of the name of the Elamite king Teumman, who backed the rebellion of Bel-Iqisha in 664 BC. Teumman's name was virtually the same as the Babylonian word tēmānu (𒌆𒈨), which meant 'wise,' suggesting that the original Neo-Assyrian story was about King Teumman and his proxy Bel-Iqisha.

3) All translations that survive to the present refer to this land as Persia, however, the Book of Tobit refers to it as Elam. This suggests that the term Persia was used in the original Aramaic translation made in the Neo-Babylonian Empire, which appears to have served for all later translations. This is historically valid, as Persia became a kingdom during the Neo-Babylonian era, and Elam no longer existed by the time that Babylon and its allies overthrew Assyria.

4) The word Nisrin, appear to be a Persian era reinterpretation of the older Neo-Assyrian cuneiform word naṣārum (𒈾𒊬𒈬). The Persian word nasrin (نسرين) means roses, while the Akkadian word meant 'protectors.' As the described geography places the Plain of Roses/Protectors in the region around Nineveh, and the Assyrians spoke Assyrian, and not Persian, the original meaning is restored.

5) All translations agree that this was Egypt, which if the previous references were to Bel-Iqisha and King Teumman in 664 BC, would make this the first regal year of Pharaoh Wahibre Psamtik I, however, at the beginning of his reign he did not control Egypt, as the Kushites had invaded and captured most of the country, and in the process killed his predecessor Pharaoh Necho I. If Nadan had sent a letter to the king of Egypt at the time it would have been King Tantamani of Kush, who was at war against Assyria. The following year, 663 BC, the Assyrian army reinvaded Egypt and drove out the Kushites, and spent the next few years occupying southern Egypt, meaning it could not have been later than 664 BC.

Words of Ahihar: Chapter 4

When the king of Egypt[1] had heard that Ahikar was dead, he rose immediately and wrote a letter to King Sennacherib, saying:

"Peace, health, might, and honor which we wish especially for you, my beloved brother, king Sennacherib.

I have been desiring to build a castle in the air between the sky and the earth, and I want you to send me a wise, clever man from yourself to build it for me, and to answer me all my questions, and that I may have the tribute and the custom duties of Assyria for three years."

Then he sealed the letter and sent it to Sennacherib, who took it and read it and gave it to his viziers and to the nobles of his kingdom, and they were confused and ashamed. He was very angry and was puzzled about how he should act. Then he assembled the old men and the learned men and the wise men and the philosophers, and the diviners and the astrologers, and everyone who was in his country, and read them the letter and said to them, "Who among you will go to Pharaoh king of Egypt and answer his riddles?"

They answered him, "Our lord king, you know that there is none in your kingdom who is acquainted with these riddles except Ahikar, your vizier and secretary. But as for us, we have no skill in this, unless it is Nadan, his sister's son, for he taught him all his wisdom and learning and knowledge. Call him to you, maybe he may untie this difficult knot."

Then the king called Nadan and said to him, "Look at this letter and understand what is in it."

When Nadan read it, he said, "My lord, who is able to build a castle in the air between the sky and the earth?"

When the king heard the question of Nadan he was very sad, and climbed down from his throne and sat in the ashes, and began to cry and wail over Ahikar saying, "My grief! Ahikar, who knew the secrets and the riddles! Woe to me, Ahikar! Teacher of my country and ruler of my kingdom, where will I find another like you? Ahikar, teacher of my country, where will I turn for you? Woe to me over you! How could I destroy you, and I listened to the talk of a stupid, ignorant boy without knowledge, without religion, without manliness. Why, and why again? Who can give you to me just for once, or bring me word that Ahikar is alive? I would give him half of my kingdom! What is this to me? Oh, Ahikar! That I might see you just once more. Oh! My grief for you, for all time! Ahikar, why have I killed you, and did not delay your case until I had seen all the information?"

The king went on weeping night and day, and when the swordsman saw the anger of the king and his sorrow for Ahikar, his heart was softened towards him, and he entered into his presence and said to him, "My lord! Command your servants to cut off my head."

Then the king asked him, "Why Abi Samik, what is your fault?"

The swordsman said to him, "My master! Every slave who acts contrary to the word of his master is killed, and I have acted contrary to your command."

Then the king asked him, "Why Abi Samik? In what way have you disobeyed my command?"

The swordsman answered him, "My lord! You commanded me to kill Ahikar, and I knew that you would have regret concerning him and that he had been wronged, and I hid him in a certain place, and I killed one of his slaves, and he is now safe in the well, and if you command me I will bring him to you."

The king said to him, "Shame on you, Abi Samik! You are mocking me and I am your lord."

The swordsman replied to him, "No, but by your life, my lord! Ahikar is safe and alive."

When the king heard this, he felt sure of the matter, and his head swam, and he fainted from joy. He commanded them to bring Ahikar. He said to the swordsman, "Trusty servant! If your words are true, I will greatly enrich you, and praise you above all your friends."

The swordsman went out rejoicing and traveled to Ahikar's house. He opened the door of the hiding-place, and went down and found Ahikar sitting, praising God, and thanking him. He called to him, saying, "Ahikar, I bring the greatest of joy, and happiness, and delight!"

Ahikar asked him, "What is the news, Abi Samik?"

He told him all about Pharaoh from the beginning to the end. Then he took him and went to the king. When the king looked at him, he saw him in a state of need, and that his hair had grown long like the wild beasts' and his nails were like the claws of an eagle, and that his body was dirty with dust, and the color of his face had changed and faded and was now like ashes. When the king saw him he was sad because of him and rose at once and embraced him and kissed him, and wept over him and said, "Praise the god who has brought you back to me."

Then he consoled him and comforted him. He stripped off his robe, and put it on the swordsman, and was very gracious to him, and gave him great wealth, and gave Ahikar peace. Then Ahikar said to the king, "Let my lord the king live forever! These are the deeds of the children of the world. I have raised a palm-tree that I might lean on it, and it bent sideways and threw me down. My lord, since I have appeared before you, don't let concerns oppress you!"

The king said to him, "Blessed is the god, who showed you mercy, and knew that you were wronged, and saved you and delivered you from being slain. Go to the warm bath, and shave your head, and cut your nails, and change your clothes, and amuse yourself for forty days, that you may be good to yourself and improve your condition and the color of your face may come back to you."

Then the king stripped off his costly robe and put it on Ahikar, and Ahikar thanked God and did obeisance to the king, and departed to his house glad and happy, praising the Highest God. The people of his household rejoiced with him, and his friends and everyone who heard that he was alive rejoiced also.

Words of Ahihar: Chapter 4 Notes

1) Assuming that the original Assyrian king in the story was Ashurbanipal, then this would have to be King Psamtik I, who ruled Egypt from 663 BC, when Ashurbanipal placed him on the throne of Egypt as an Assyrian vassal to 610 BC, several decades after the fall of Assyria. There are no surviving records of him attempting to build a castle in the sky, or anything else of significance. Most of his reign seems to have been focused on military campaigns and politics. He managed to defend Egypt from any further Kushite incursions, and successfully transitioned the country from being an Assyrian vassal to an independent nation. After Assyria fell, he spent the next few couple of decades competing with the Babylonians for control of Canaan.

Words of Ahihar: Chapter 5

He did as the king commanded him, and rested for forty days. Then he dressed himself in his nicest clothes, and rode to the king, with his slaves behind him and before him, rejoicing and delighted. But when Nadan saw what was happening, fear took hold of him and terror, and he was confused, not knowing what to do.

When Ahikar saw it he entered into the king's presence and greeted him, and he returned the greeting, and made him sit down at his side, saying to him, "My friend Ahikar! Look at these letters which the king of Egypt sent to us after he heard that you were killed. They have provoked us and confused us, and many of the people of our country have fled to Egypt in fear of the tribute that the king of Egypt has demanded from us."

Then Ahikar took the letter and read it, and understood its contents. Then he said to the king, "Do not be angry, my lord! I will go to Egypt, and I will return the answers to Pharaoh, and I will display this letter to him, and I will reply to him about the tribute, and I will send back all those who have run away, and I will put your enemies to shame with the help of the Highest God, and for the happiness of your kingdom."

When the king heard this speech from Ahikar he rejoiced greatly, and his heart was expanded and he showed him favor. Ahikar asked the king, "Grant me a delay of forty days that I may consider this question and answer it."

The king permitted this, and Ahikar returned to his home. He commanded the hunters to capture two young eagles for him, and they captured them and brought them to him. He commanded the weavers of ropes to weave two cotton ropes for him, each two thousand cubits long. He had the carpenters brought to him and ordered them to make two great boxes, which they did. Then he took two young boys, and spent every day sacrificing lambs, and feeding the eagles and the boys. He made the boys ride on the backs of the eagles, and he bound them with a firm knot, and tied the cable to the feet of the eagles, and let them soar upwards little by little every day, to a distance of ten cubits, until they grew used to it and were trained to do it. They rose all the length of the rope until they reached the sky, with the boys on their backs. Then he pulled them back to himself.

When Ahikar saw that his plan was working he ordered the boys that when they were carried up into the sky, they were to shout, "Bring us clay and stone, so we can build a castle for king Pharaoh, as we are idle."

Ahikar was never done training them and exercising them until they had reached the highest possible place.

Then leaving them he went to the king and said to him, "My lord! The work is finished as to your desire. Rise with me that I may show you the wonder."

So the king got up and sat with Ahikar and went to a wide place and sent to bring the eagles and the boys, and Ahikar tied them and let them up into the air all the length of the ropes, and they began to shout as he had taught them. Then he drew them to himself and put them in their places. The king and those who were with him wondered greatly, and the king kissed Ahikar between his eyes and said to him, "Go in peace, my friend, pride of my kingdom, to Egypt and answer the riddles of Pharaoh and overcome him by the strength of the Highest God."

Then he commanded him farewell, and took his troops and his army and the young men and the eagles, and went towards the dwellings of Egypt, and when he had arrived, he turned towards the country of the king.

When the people of Egypt knew that Sennacherib had sent a man of his trusted council to talk with Pharaoh and to answer his questions, they took the news to king Pharaoh, and he sent a party of his trusted councilors to bring him before him.

He came and entered into the presence of Pharaoh, and did obeisance to him as it is fitting to do to kings, and he said to him, "My lord the king, Sennacherib the king hails you with abundance of peace and might, and honor. He has sent me, who is one of his servants, that I may answer you your questions, and may fulfill all your desire, for you have sent a message to my lord the king seeking a man who will build you a castle between the sky and the earth. I, through the help of the Highest God and your noble favor and the power of my lord the king will build it for you as you desire. But, my lord king, what you have said about the tribute of Egypt for three years, now the stability of a kingdom is strict justice, and if you win and my hand has no skill in replying to you, then my lord the king will send you the tribute which you have mentioned. If I will have answered you in your questions, it will remain for you to send whatever you have mentioned to my lord the king."

When Pharaoh heard that speech, he wondered and was perplexed by the freedom of his tongue and the pleasantness of his speech. King Pharaoh asked him, "Man, what is your name?"

He answered, "Your servant is Abi Qam, and I am but a little ant among the ants of King Sennacherib."

Pharaoh said to him, "Has your lord no one of higher dignity than you, that he has sent me a little ant to reply to me, and to talk with me?"

Ahikar said to him, "My lord king! I will pray to God Highest that I may fulfill what is on your mind, for God is with the weak that he may confound the strong."

Then Pharaoh commanded that they should prepare a living place for Abi Qam and supply him with provisions, meat, and drink, and all that he needed. When it was finished, three days afterward Pharaoh clothed himself in purple and red and sat on his throne, and all his viziers and the magnates of his kingdom were standing with their hands crossed, their feet close together, and their heads bowed.

Pharaoh sent to fetch Abi Qam, and when he was presented to him, he did obeisance before him, and kissed the ground in front of him. King Pharaoh asked him, "Abi Qam, who am I like? And the nobles of my kingdom, who are they like?"

Ahikar answered him, "My lord king, you are like the god Bel, and the nobles of your kingdom are like his servants."

He said to him, "Go, and come back here tomorrow."

So Ahikar left as king Pharaoh had commanded him. In the morning, Ahikar returned into the presence of Pharaoh, and did obeisance, and stood before the king. Pharaoh was dressed in a red, and the nobles were dressed in white. Pharaoh asked him, "Abi Qam, who am

I like? And the nobles of my kingdom, who are they like?"

Ahikar answered him, "My lord, you are like the sun, and your servants are like its beams."

Pharaoh replied to him, "Go to your home, and return here tomorrow."

Then Pharaoh commanded his court to wear pure white, and Pharaoh was dressed like them and sat on his throne, and he commanded them to fetch Ahikar. He entered and sat down before him, and Pharaoh asked him, "Abi Qam, who am I like? And my nobles, who are they like?"

Abi Qam answered him, "My lord, you are like the moon, and your nobles are like the planets and the stars."

Pharaoh replied to him, "Go, and tomorrow return here."

Then Pharaoh commanded his servants to wear robes of various colors, and Pharaoh wore a red velvet dress, and sat on his throne, and commanded them to bring in Abi Qam. He entered and did obeisance before him, and he asked, "Abi Qam, who am I like? And my armies, who are they like?"

He answered, "My lord, you are like the month of Parmouti,[1] and your armies are like its flowers."

WORDS OF AHIHAR: CHAPTER 5

When the king heard it he rejoiced greatly and said, "The first time you compared me to the idol Bel, and my nobles to his servants. The second time you compared me to the sun, and my nobles to the sunbeams. The third time you compared me to the moon, and my nobles to the planets and the stars. The fourth time you compared me to the month of Parmouti, and my nobles to its flowers. But now, Abi Qam, tell me, your lord King Sennacherib, who is he like? And his nobles, who are they like?"

Ahikar shouted with a loud voice and said, "It is far from me to make mention of my lord the king, while you are seated on your throne. Get up on your feet that I may tell you who my lord the king is like and who his nobles are like."

Pharaoh was confused by the freedom of his words and his boldness in answering. Pharaoh rose from his throne, and stood before Ahikar, and said, "Tell me now, that I may know who your lord the king is like, and who his nobles are like."

Ahikar said to him, "My lord is the sky god, and his nobles are the lightning and the thunder, and when he wills it, the winds blow and the rain falls. He commands the thunder, and there is lightning and rain, and he holds the Sun, and it does not give its light, and the moon and the stars, and they don't circle. He commands the tempest, and it blows and the rain falls and it tramples in Parmouti and destroys its flowers and its houses."

When Pharaoh heard this speech, he was very confused and was extremely angry, and said to him, "Man, tell me the truth, and let me know who you really are."

He admitted the truth, "I am Ahikar the scribe, greatest of the trusted councilors of King Sennacherib, and I am his vizier and the governor of his kingdom, and his chancellor."

He said to him, "You have told the truth in this saying. But we have heard that king Sennacherib has executed Ahikar, yet you seem to be alive and well."

Ahikar answered him, "Yes, so it was, but praise be to God, who knows what is hidden, for my lord the king commanded me to be killed, and he believed the lies told of men, but the Lord saved me, and blessed is he who trusts in him."

Pharaoh said to Ahikar, "Go, and tomorrow return here, and tell me something that I have never heard from my nobles or the people of my kingdom and my country."

Words of Ahihar: Chapter 5 Notes

1) Greek: Pharmouthi (Φαρμουθί)

- Armenian: Pôarmutôi (Փարմութի)
- Arabic: Baramūdah (برموده)

På-en-renen-wetet (𓊪𓈖𓂋𓈖𓏲𓏏𓏏𓆗) was the eight month of the Egyptian civil calendar, and the last month of the Season of the Emergence (𓉐𓂋𓏏𓊖), when the Nile floods receded and the crops started to grow. It continued into the Coptic calendars as Parmouti (Παρμογτε) and Tharmouthi (Φαρμογθι). This month is approximately April 9 to May 8 on the Gregorian calendar during the 21st-century. It is generally translated as Parmouti in English from the Sahidic dialect of Coptic.

Words of Ahihar: Chapter 6

Ahikar returned to his residence, and wrote a letter, saying in it on this:

"From King Sennacherib of Nineveh in Assyria to Pharaoh king of Egypt.

Peace be on you, my brother!

Let us make known to you through this message that a brother needs his brother, and kings of each other, and my hope from you is that you would lend me nine hundred talents of gold, for I need it for the provisioning of some of the soldiers, and I will spend it on them. At some point, I will return it to you."

Then he folded the letter and presented it in the morning to Pharaoh. When he saw it, he was confused and said to him, "I have never heard anything like these words from anyone."

Then Ahikar said to him, "Truly this is a debt which you owe to my lord the king."

Pharaoh accepted this, saying, "Ahikar, it is your way to be honest in the service of kings. Blessed be God who has made you perfect in wisdom and has adorned you with philosophy and knowledge. Now, Ahikar, there remains what we desire from you, that you should build as a castle between the sky and earth."

Then Ahikar replied, "To hear is to obey. I will build you a castle as you wish, but, my lord I will need lime, stone, clay, and workmen prepared. I have skilled builders who will build it for you as you desire."

The king prepared everything for him, and they went to a wide place where Ahikar also came, and he took the eagles and the young boys with him. The king and all his nobles went and the whole city assembled, that they might see what Ahikar would do. Then Ahikar let the eagles out of the boxes, and tied the young men on their backs, and tied the ropes to the eagles' feet, and let them go in the air. They soared upwards, till they were between the sky and earth.

The boys began to shout, saying, "Bring bricks, bring clay, that we may build the king's castle, for we are standing idle!"

The crowd was astonished and perplexed, and they wondered. The king and his nobles wondered. Ahikar and his servants began to beat the workmen, and they shouted for the king's troops, saying to them, "Bring the skilled workmen what they want and do not stop them from their work."

The king said to him, "You are mad, who can bring anything up to that height?"

Ahikar said to him, "My lord, how will we build a castle in the air? If my lord the king were here, he would have built several castles in a single day."

Pharaoh said to him, "Leave Ahikar, to your residence, and rest. We have given up building the castle, but tomorrow return to me."

Then Ahikar went to his residence and in the morning he returned to Pharaoh, and Pharaoh said, "Ahikar, what news is there of the horse of your lord? When he neighs in Nineveh in the country of Assyria, and our mares hear his voice, they abandon their young."

When Ahikar heard this riddle he went and took a cat, and tied her up and began to flog her violently until the Egyptians heard it, and they went and told the king about it. Pharaoh sent for Ahikar, and said to him, "Ahikar, why do you flog and beat that dumb animal?"

Ahikar said to him, my lord the king, she has done an ugly deed to me and has deserved this beating and flogging, for my lord King Sennacherib had given me a fine rooster, and he had a strong true voice and knew the hours of the day and the night. The cat got up this very night and bit off its head and went away, and because of this deed I have beaten her."

Pharaoh said to him, "Ahikar, I see from all this that you are growing old and are losing your mind, for between Egypt and Nineveh there are sixty-eight leagues,[1] and how did she go this very night and cut off the head of your rooster and returned?"

Ahikar said to him, "My lord, if there is such a distance between Egypt and Nineveh how could your mares hear when my lord the king's horse neighs and abandon their young? How could the voice of the horse reach Egypt?"

When Pharaoh heard that, he knew that Ahikar had answered his riddle, and Pharaoh said, "Ahikar, I want you to make me ropes from the sea-sand."

Ahikar said to him, "My lord king, order them to bring me a rope out of the treasury that I may make one like it."

Then Ahikar went to the back of the house, and drilled holes in the rough shape of the sea, and took a handful of sand in his hand, sea-sand. When the sun rose and shone through the holes, he spread the sand in the sun till it looked like woven like ropes. Ahikar said, "Command your servants to take these ropes, and whenever you desire it, I will weave you some more like them."

Pharaoh said, "Ahikar, we have a millstone here and it has been broken and I want you to sew it up."

Then Ahikar looked at it and found another stone. He said, "My lord, I am a foreigner, and I have no tool for sewing. But I want you to command your faithful shoe-makers to cut awls from this stone, that I may sew that millstone."

Then Pharaoh and all his nobles laughed. He said, "Blessed be the Highest God, who gave you this wit and knowledge."

When Pharaoh saw that Ahikar had overcome him, and answered his riddles, he at once became excited and commanded them to collect for him three years' tribute and to bring them to Ahikar. He stripped off his robes and put them on Ahikar, and his soldiers, and his servants, and gave him the expenses of his journey. He said to him, "Go in peace, strength of your lord and pride of your teachers. Does any king have one like you? Give my greetings to your lord King Sennacherib, and say to him how we have sent him gifts, for kings are content with little."

Then Ahikar arose, and kissed king Pharaoh's hands and kissed the ground in front of him, and wished him strength and continuance, and abundance in his treasury, and said to him, "My lord, I desire from you that not one of our countrymen may remain in Egypt."

Pharaoh rose and sent heralds to proclaim in the streets of Egypt that not one of the people of Nineveh in Assyria should remain in the land of Egypt, but that they should go with Ahikar. Then Ahikar left King

Pharaoh and traveled to Nineveh in the land of Assyria and he had some treasures and a great deal of wealth.

When the news reached King Sennacherib that Ahikar was coming, he went out to meet him and rejoiced over him exceedingly with great joy and embraced him and kissed him and said to him, "Welcome home, my relative, my brother Ahikar, the strength of my kingdom, and pride of my realm. Ask what you would have from me, even if you desire half of my kingdom and my possessions."

Then Ahikar said to him, "My lord king, live forever! Show favor, my lord king, to Abi Samik instead of me, for my life was in the hands of God and also his."

Then King Sennacherib said, "Honor be to you, my beloved Ahikar! I will make the station of Abi Samik the swordsman, higher than all my trusted councilors and my favorites."

Then the king began to ask him how he had dealt with Pharaoh from when he arrived until he had left his presence, and how he had answered all his questions, and how he had received the tribute from him, and the changes of clothing and the presents. King Sennacherib celebrated with great joy, and said to Ahikar, "Take what you would have of this tribute, for it is all within your hands."

Ahikar replied, "Let the king live forever! I desire nothing but the safety of my lord king and the continuance of his greatness. My lord, what can I do with wealth and its like? But if you will show me favor, give me Nadan, my sister's son, that I may repay him for what he has done to me, and grant me his blood and hold me guiltless of it."

Sennacherib the king said, "Take him, I have given him to you."

Ahikar took Nadan, his sister's son, and bound his hands with chains of iron, and took him to his home, and put heavy shackles on his feet, and tied it with a tight knot, and after binding him so he threw him into a dark room, beside the retiring-place, and appointed Nebu-hal as watchman over him to give him a loaf of bread and a little water every day.

Words of Ahihar: Chapter 6 Notes

1) Aramaic: pŕshå (**ΝΠℨᗰ)**). Translation: parasang (or league)

• Greek: parasángēs (παρασάγγης). Translation: parasang (or league)

• Armenian: hrasax (Հրասախ). Translation: parasang (or league)

• Arabic: farsak (فَرْسَخ). Translation: parasang (or league)

The unit of measurement used in the text was the parasang, a Persian unit that was adopted by many other cultures. The term is accepted as having been adopted by other cultures during the Persian era, meaning it must have been a Persian era replacement for an older term. Its length was not consistent, ranging between 4.8 and 5.6 km (3 to 3½ miles). The term could not have been the original term in the text, as 68 parasangs would have only been about 340 km (200 miles), while the distance from the Egyptian capital of Sais to Nineveh would have been 1500 to 1600 kilometers (900 to 1000 miles), depending on the route taken.

The earlier Mesopotamian unit of measurement which is also translated into English as 'league,' was the bêr (𒁰𒆳𒂀), which was approximately 2.7 km (1.7 miles) long, even shorter than the parasang. The text implies that the original unit of measurement that the king of Egypt used, was very long as there were only 68 of them between Egypt and Assyria. The longest Egyptian unit of measurement that appears to have been used at the time was the jtrw (𓇋𓏏𓂋𓈖𓏴), which is translated into English as the 'River-Measure League,' as it was a nautical distance. It was approximately 10.5 km (6.5 miles) long, which would make the distance listed approximately 714 km (444 miles), which is only half the distance from Sais to Nineveh. As the unit of measurement was nautical, and the distance mentioned was approximately the distance from Sais to the Assyrian ports in Lebanon, it is plausible that the original text was referring to the Assyrian Empire, and not the city of Nineveh itself.

Words of Ahihar: Chapter 7

Whenever Ahikar went in or out, he chastised Nadan, his sister's son, saying, "Nadan, my boy, I have done to you all that is good and kind and you have rewarded me for it, with what is ugly and bad and with murder. My son, it is said in the proverbs, 'He who does not listen with his ears, they will make listen with the scruff of his neck.'"

Nadan asked, "Why are you angry with me?"

Ahikar said to him, "Because I raised you, and taught you, and gave you honor and respect and made you great, and reared you with the best of breeding, and seated you in my place that you might be my heir in the world, and you treated me with killing and repaid me with my ruin. But the Lord knew that I was wronged, and he saved me from the trap which you had set for me, for the Lord heals the broken hearts and hinders the envious and the haughty.

My boy, you have been to me like the scorpion which when it strikes on brass, pierces it.

My boy, you are like the gazelle who was eating the roots of the madder, and it adds to me today, but tomorrow they will tan they hide in my roots.

My boy, you have been like he who saw his comrade naked in the winter, and he took cold water and poured it on him.

My boy, you have been to me like a man who took a stone and threw it up to the sky to stone the Lord with it. The stone did not hit and did not reach high enough, but it became the cause of guilt and sin.

My boy, if you had honored me and respected me and had listened to my words you would have been my heir and would have reigned over my dominions.

My son, know that if the tail of the dog or the pig were ten cubits long it would not approach the worth of the horse's even if it were like silk.

My boy! I thought that you would have been my heir at my death, and you through your envy and your insolence desired to kill me. But the Lord delivered me from your cunning.

My son, you have been to me like a trap which was set up on the dunghill, and there came a sparrow and found the trap set up. The sparrow asked the trap, "Why are you here?"

The trap answered, "I am praying here to God."

The lark also asked it, "What is the piece of wood that you hold?"

The trap replied, "That is a young oak-tree on which I lean at the time of prayer."

The lark asked, "What is that thing in your mouth?"

The trap answered, "That is bread and meat which I carry for all the hungry and the poor who come near to me."

The lark asked, "Now then, may I come forward and eat, as I am hungry?"

The trap answered him, "Come forward."

The lark approached so it might eat, but the trap sprang up and seized the lark by its neck. The lark answered and said to the trap, "If that is your bread for the hungry God will not accept your alms and your kind deeds. If that is your fasting and your prayers, God accepts from you neither your fast or your prayer, and God will not perfect what is good concerning you."

My boy, you have been to me like a lion who made friends with a donkey, and the donkey kept walking before the lion for a time, and one day the lion sprang on the donkey and ate it up.

My boy, you have been to me like a weevil in the wheat, for it does nothing good, but spoils the wheat and eats it.

My boy, you have been like a man who sowed ten measures of wheat, and when it was harvest time, he arose and reaped it, and separated it, and threshed it, and struggled over it to the utmost, and it turned out to be ten measures, and its master said to it, "You lazy thing, you have not grown and you have not shrunk."

My boy, you have been to me like the partridge that had been thrown into the net, and she could not save herself, but she called out to the partridges, that she might get them caught in the net with her.

My son, you have been to me like the cold dog and it went into the potter's house to get warm. When it had gotten warm, it began to bark at them, and they chased it out and beat it, that it might not bite them.

My son, you have been to me like the pig who went into the hot bath with people of quality, and when it came out of the hot bath, it saw a muddy hole and it went down and wallowed in it.

My son, you have been to me like the goat which joined its comrades on their way to the sacrifice, and it was unable to save itself.

My boy, the dog which is not fed through its hunting becomes food for flies.

My son, the hand which does not labor and plow and is greedy and cunning will be cut away from its shoulder.

My son, the eye in which light is not seen, the ravens will pick at it and pluck it out.

My boy, you have been to me like a tree whose branches they were cutting, and it said to them, "If something of me were not in your hands, verily you would be unable to cut me."

My boy, you are like the cat to who they said, "Stop stealing until we make you a chain of gold and feed you with sugar and almonds."

She replied, "I am not forgetful of the craft of my father and my mother."

My son, you have been like the serpent riding on a thorn-bush when he was among a river, and a wolf saw them and said, "Mischief on mischief, and let him who is more mischievous than they direct both of them."

The serpent said to the wolf, "The lambs and the goats and the sheep which you have eaten all your life, will you return them to their fathers and their parents or not?"

The wolf answered, "No."

The serpent said to him, "I think that after myself you are the worst of us."

My boy, I fed you with good food and you did not feed me with dry bread.

My boy, I gave you sugared water to drink and good syrup, and you did not give me water from the well to drink.

My boy, I taught you and raised you, and you dug a hiding-place for me and hid me.

My boy, I brought you up with the best upbringing and trained you like a tall cedar, and you have twisted and bent me.

My boy, it was my hope concerning you that you would build me a fortified castle, that I might be concealed from my enemies in it, and you did become to me like one buried in the depth of the earth, but the Lord took pity on me and delivered me from your cunning.

My boy, I wished you well, and you did reward me with evil and hatefulness, and now I would fain tear from your eyes, and make you food for dogs, and cut out your tongue, and take off your head with the edge of the sword, and repay you for your abominable deeds."

When Nadan heard this speech from his uncle Ahikar, he said, "My uncle! Deal with me according to your knowledge, and forgive my sins, for who is there who has sinned like me, or who is there who forgives like you? Accept me, my uncle! Now I will serve in your house, and groom your horses and sweep up the dung of your livestock, and feed your sheep, for I am wicked and you are righteous. I the guilty and you the forgiving."

Ahikar answered him, "My boy, you are like the tree which was fruitless beside the water, and its master decided to cut it down, and it said to him, 'Move me to another place, and if I do not carry fruit, cut me down.'

Its master said to it, 'You've been beside the water and have not borne fruit, how will you carry fruit when you are in another place?'

My boy, the old age of the eagle is better than the youth of the crow.

My boy, they told the wolf, 'Keep away from the sheep in case their dust should harm you.' The wolf said, 'The dregs of the sheep's milk are good for my eyes.'

My boy, they made the wolf go to a school so he might learn to read and they said to him, 'Say A, B...' He said, 'Lamb, goat...'

My boy, they set the donkey down at the table and he fell and began to roll himself in the dust and one said,

"Let him roll himself, for it is his nature, he will not change."

My boy, the saying has been confirmed which goes, 'If you beget a boy, call him your son, and if you teach a boy, call him your slave.'

My boy, he who does good, will meet with good; and he who does evil will meet with evil, for the Lord repays a man according to the measure of his work.

My boy, what will I say more to you than these sayings? The Lord knows what is hidden, and is acquainted with the mysteries and the secrets. He will repay you and will judge, between me and you, and will repay you according to all your deserve."

When Nadan heard that speech from his uncle Ahikar, he swelled up immediately and became like a blown-out canteen. His limbs swelled and his legs and his feet and his side, and he was torn and his belly burst and his intestines were scattered, and he died. His end was destruction, and he went to the grave. For he who digs a pit for his brother will fall into it, and he who sets up traps will be caught in them.

This is what happened and what we found about the Words of Ahikar. Praise God forever. Amen, and peace.

This chronicle is finished with the help of God, may he be praised! Amen, Amen, Amen.

Ahihar Restoration: Chapter 1

This is the story of Ahikar[1] the sage, vizier of King Ashurbanipal,[2] and of Ahikar's nephew Nadan.[3]

There was a vizier in the days of King Ashurbanipal, son of King Esarhaddon[4] of Nineveh in Assyria, a wise man named Ahikar. He had a great fortune and a great deal of property, and he was skillful, wise, a philosopher in knowledge, and opinionated in government. He had married sixty women and had built a mansion for each of them. Yet he had no child by any of these women who could be his heir. He was very sad on account of this, and one day he assembled the astrologers and the learned men and the wizards and explained to them his condition and the matter of his barrenness. They said to him, "Go, sacrifice to the gods and beg them, maybe they will provide you with a son."

He did as they told him and offered sacrifices to the idols, and prayed to them and begged them with requests. They did not answer him even one word. He went away sad and dejected, departing with a pain at his heart. He returned and implored the Highest God,[5] and believed, begging him with a burning in his heart, saying, "Highest God, creator of the skies and the earth, creator of all created things! I beg you to give me a son, that I may be consoled by him, and that he may be present in my home, and that he may close my eyes, and that he may bury me."

Then there came to him a voice saying, "As you have relied first of all on carved statues, and have offered sacrifices to them, for this reason, you will remain childless your whole life. But adopt Nadan your sister's son, and make him your child and teach him what you've learned and your good breeding, and at your death, he will bury you."

Thereafter he took Nadan his sister's son, who was still an infant. He handed him over to eight wet-nurses, that they might suckle him and raise him. They raised him with good food and gentle training and silk clothing, and purple and crimson, and he was seated on couches of silk. When Nadan grew big and walked, shooting up like a tall cedar, he taught him good manners and writing and science and philosophy.

After many days King Ashurbanipal looked at Ahikar and saw that he had grown very old, and he said to him, "My honored friend, the skillful, trustworthy, wise governor, my secretary, my vizier, my chancellor, and director. You have grown very old and weighted with years, and your departure from this world must be near. Tell me who will have a place in my service after you."

Ahikar said to him, "My lord, may you live forever! There is Nadan my sister's son, I have adopted him as my child. I have brought him up and taught him my wisdom and knowledge."

The king said to him, "Ahikar, bring him into my presence so I may see him, and if I find him suitable put him in your place, and you will go your way, to take a rest and to live the remainder of your life in sweet repose."

Then Ahikar went and presented Nadan his sister's son. He paid homage and wished him power and honor. He looked at him and admired him and rejoiced in him and said to Ahikar, "Is this your son, Ahikar? I pray that God may preserve him. As you have served me and my father Esarhaddon so may this boy of your serve me and fulfill my desires, needs, and business, so that I may honor him and make him powerful for your sake."

Ahikar paid obeisance to the king and said to him, "May you live forever, my lord king! I ask you that you may be patient with my boy Nadan and forgive his mistakes, so he may serve you as it is fitting."

Then the king swore to him that he would make him the greatest of his favorites, and the most powerful of his friends and that he should be with him in all honor and respect. He kissed his hands and bid him farewell. He took Nadan, his sister's son with him and seated him in a parlor and set about teaching him night and day until he had filled him with wisdom and knowledge more than with bread and water.

Ahihar Restoration: Chapter 1 Notes

1) Aramaic: Åhyqr (ק/^חת^רק)

- Greek: Achiacharos (Αχιαχαρος)

- Armenian Xikar (Խիկար)

- Arabic: Ḥayqār (حَيْقَار)

- Old Slavonic: Akyrios (ꚠ꙼Ꙥ·ꙗꙗ)

The variations of the name Ahikar transliterated into various translations of the book indicate that most copies were made from the Aramaic version of the book. The Codex Sinaiticus' Tobit, chapter 11 also includes a direct translation of the Aramaic name as Achicar (Αχικαρ), confirming that the Aramaic translation of Tobit used the same name for him.

2) Aramaic: Snhryb (ﬤ^רﬣ^ﬡﬤ)

- Greek: Sanacharibos (Σαναχάριβος)

- Armenian: Sinak'erib (Uһūաքերիµ)

- Arabic: Snhāryb (سنحاريب)

King Sîn-ahhī-erība (𒀭𒌍𒉺𒂠) was the king of the Assyrian Empire between 705 and 681 BC. While all surviving versions of the Words of Ahikar agree that it was Sennacherib, the actual successor to Esarhaddon was Ashurbanipal, indicating that the name of Ashurbanipal was redacted. The oldest copy of the book, an Aramaic copy that had been in use at the Israelite Temple of Elephantine used the name Bel where the later translations substituted 'God' or 'Lord,' indicating that the Aramaic translation was created in the Neo-Babylonian Empire, explaining why Ashurbanipal's name was removed from the text. Ashurbanipal devastated Babylonia and Elam during the civil/international war against his brother Shamash-shum-ukin and his allies in Elam in the 640s BC. The Assyrians won the war, but at such a tremendous financial cost, and with such a loss of prestige, that Nabopolassar was able to lead another Babylonian revolt in the 620s BC, a few years after Ashurbanipal's death. This rebellion drew in virtually all of Assyria's neighbors, and ultimately destroyed the Neo-Assyrian Empire, dividing its territory between the newly independent Neo-Babylonian Empire, the Median Empire, and the Lydian Empire. When the Aramaic version of Ahikar was translated, Ashurbanipal would have been seen in a similar light to how Hitler was viewed after the Second World War, making his redaction from the text a necessity.

Additionally, Ahikar could not have worked for Sennacherib, who was one of the Assyrian Kings that conquered his homeland of Samaria and exiled his people. Sennacherib would not have sent a Samaritan captive to represent him in negotiations in Egypt or Elam. The Book of Tobit recorded that both Tobit and Ahikar worked for Esarhaddon, however, Ahikar was Tobit's nephew, and therefore would have continued to work for Esarhaddon's successor Ashurbanipal. Unfortunately, all known copies of Ahikar are based on the Aramaic translation, and therefore include this anachronism.

3) Aramaic: Ndn (𐤍𐤃𐤍)

- Greek: Nadab (Ναβαδ)

- Armenian: Nadin (Նադհու)

- Arabic: Nbāb (نباب)

Nadan's name is not standardized, and appears to have diverged during the Persian era. This translation uses the Aramaic variant of Ndn, which is probably the original, and certainly served as the

227

source for the Armenian variant of Nadin. The Greek of Nabab and Arabic variant of Nbāb, probably reflect a Persian era Moabite reinterpretation within the Aramaic versions of Ahikar. Ndb (𐤍𐤃𐤁) was a Moabite word meaning 'willing,' and often used in religious context for one who is 'willing to serve a god,' such as the name Chemosh-nadab (𐤊𐤌𐤔𐤍𐤃𐤁), a Moabite king who agreed to pay tribute to Assyria after Sennacherib's Levantine Wars.

4) Aramaic: Åsrḥdwn (𐤀𐤎𐤓𐤇𐤃𐤍)

• Greek: Esarhaddon (Εσαρχαδδών)

• Arabic: Åsrḥdwn (آسرحدون)

Aššur-aḫa-iddina, more commonly known as Esarhaddon from the Hebrew version of his name Ēsar-ḥaddōn (אֵסַר־חַדֹּן) was actually Sennacherib's son, not his father. Esarhaddon was the king of the Assyrian Empire between 681 and 669 BC. He is famous for conquering Egypt and creating the largest Empire in Middle-eastern history until then.

5) The Highest is a reference to God, or a god, found in many ancient religions in the region. According to the Torah, the ancient people of Jerusalem worshiped El elyovn (אֵל עֶלְיֹון), which translates as 'God highest' when Abraham passed through the region. The Greeks translated it as theô tô ypsistô (Θεω τω υψιστω) in the Septuagint, also meaning 'God the highest.' El elyovn is known to have been a major god of the Canaanites, called ål wålyn (𐤏𐤋𐤉𐤍 𐤀𐤋), meaning 'God and highest' in an Aramaic language Sefire Treaty from circa 750 BC.

The Greek translations of Sanchuniathon's bronze age writing that have survived to the present, referred to the primordial creator god of the Canaanites as Elioun (Ελιουν), which appears to be the same god. According to Sanchuniathon, Elioun was the 'highest' (υψιστος) god, who made the sky and the land, and they made the rest of the gods. While the many references to Bel in this text appear to refer to the Babylonian god Bel, these references to the Highest are clearly references to the old Canaanite god El elyovn. A version of El elyovn was worshiped by the Neo-Assyrians in the form of ^{deity}Šar (𒀭𒊹), more commonly called Anshar today. Anshar translates directly as 'deity totality' or 'deity eternity,' and was perceived in the later Neo-Assyrian era as the patriarch of the gods who created everything.

Ahihar Restoration: Chapter 2

He taught him, saying, "My son! Hear my speech and follow my advice and remember what I say.

My son, if you hear a word, let it remain in your heart, and don't reveal it to another, in case it becomes a lump of burning coal and burns your tongue and causes pain in your body, and you become reproachful and are shamed before God and man.

My son, if you have heard a report, don't spread it, and if you have seen something, don't tell it.

My son, make your speech easy to the listener and do not rush to answer questions.

My son, when you have heard anything, don't hide it.

My son, don't loosen a sealed knot, or untie it, and don't seal a loosened knot.

My son, don't covet outward beauty, for it fades and passes away, but instead an honorable memory that lasts forever.

My son, don't let a foolish woman deceive you with her speech, in case you die the most miserable of deaths, and she entangles you in a net until you are trapped.

My son, don't desire a woman beautified with clothing and with ointments, who is despicable and foolish in her mind. Woe to you if you bestow on her anything that is yours or commit to her what is in your hand and she entices you into sin, and God becomes angry with you.

My son, do not be like the almond-tree, for it brings out leaves before all the trees, and edible fruit after them all, but be like the mulberry-tree, which brings out edible fruit before all the trees, and leaves after them all.

My son, bend your head low down, and soften your voice, and be courteous, and walk in the straight path, and don't be foolish. Don't raise your voice when you laugh for if it were by a loud voice that a house was built, the donkey would build many houses every day, and if it were just through strength that the plow was driven, the plow would never be removed from under the shoulders of the camels.

My son, the moving of stones with a wise man is better than the drinking of wine with a foolish man.

My son, pour out your wine on the tombs of the just and don't drink with ignorant, contemptible people.

My son, cling to wise men who fear God and be like them, and don't go near the ignorant, in case you become like him and learn his ways.

My son, when you have a comrade or a friend, test him, and afterward make him a comrade and a friend, and do not praise him without testing him. Do not waste your speech with a man who lacks wisdom.

My son, while a shoe stays on your foot, walk with it on the thorns, and make a road for your son, and for your household and your children, and make your ship taut before she goes on the sea and its waves and sinks and cannot be saved.

My son, if the rich man eats a snake, they say, "It is through his wisdom," and if a poor man eats it, the people say, "Because he is hungry."

My son, be content with your daily bread and your goods and don't covet what is another's.

My son, don't be neighbor to the fool, and don't eat bread with him, and don't rejoice in the calamities of your neighbors. If your enemy wrongs you, show him kindness.

My son, a man who fears God, fears him and honors him.

My son, the ignorant man falls and stumbles, and the wise man, even if he stumbles is not shaken, and even if he falls, he gets up quickly, and if he is sick he can take care of his life. But as for the ignorant, stupid man, there is no drug for his disease.

My son, if a man approaches you who is inferior to yourself, go forward to meet him and remain on your feet. If he cannot repay you, his lord will repay you for him.

My son, don't spare beating your son, for the beating of your son is like manure to the garden, and like tying the opening of a purse, and like the tethering of beasts, and like the bolting of the door.

My son, restrain your son from wickedness, and teach him manners before he rebels against you and brings you into contempt among the people and you hang your head in the streets and the assemblies and you be punished for the evil of his wicked deeds.

My son, get a fat ox with a foreskin, and a donkey with great hoofs, and don't get an ox with large horns, or make friends with a deceitful man, or get a quarrelsome slave, or a thievish handmaid, for everything which you give to them they will ruin.

My son, don't let your parents curse you, and the Lord[1] be pleased with them, for it has been said, "He who despises his father or his mother, let him die the death and he who honors his parents will prolong his days and his life and will see all that is good."

My son, don't travel the road without weapons, for you don't know when a foe may meet you, and you should be ready for him.

My son, do not be like a bare, leafless tree that does not grow, but be like a tree covered with its leaves and its boughs, for the man who has neither wife nor children is disgraced in the world and is hated by them, like a leafless and fruitless tree.

My son, be like a fruitful tree on the roadside, whose fruit is eaten by all who pass by, and the beasts of the desert rest under its shade and eat of its leaves.

My son, every sheep that wanders from its path and its companions becomes food for the wolf.

My son, don't say, "My lord is a fool and I am wise," and don't relate the speech of ignorance and folly, in case you become hated by him.

My son, don't be one of those servants, to who their lords say, "Get away from us," but be one of those to whom they say, "Approach and come near to us."

My son, don't caress your slave in the presence of his companion, for you don't know which of them will be of most value to you in the end.

My son, don't be afraid of the Lord who created you, in case he is silent to you.

My son, make your speech fair and sweeten your tongue, and don't let your companion step on your foot, in case at another time he steps on your chest.

My son, if you defeat a wise man with a word of wisdom, it will lurk in his chest like a subtle sense of shame, but if you beat the ignorant with a stick he will neither understand nor hear.

My son, if you send a wise man for your needs, do not give him many orders, for he will do your business as you desire, and if you send a fool, do not order him, but go yourself and do your business, for if you order him, he will not do what you desire. If they send you on business, hurry to fulfill it quickly.

My son, don't make an enemy of a man stronger than yourself, for he will take your measure, and his revenge on you.

My son, test your son, and your servant, before you trust your belongings to them, in case they run away with them, for he who has a full hand is called wise, even if he is stupid and ignorant, and he who has an empty hand is called poor and ignorant, even if he is the prince of sages.

My son, I have eaten colocynth,[2] and swallowed bitters, and I have found nothing more bitter than poverty and scarcity.

My son, teach your son frugality and hunger, that he may do well in the management of his household.

My son, don't teach the ignorant the language of wise men, for it will be burdensome to him.

My son, don't display your condition to your friend, in case you become despised by him.

My son, the blindness of the heart is more terrible than the blindness of the eyes, for the blindness of the eyes may be guided little by little, but the blindness of the heart is not guided, and it leaves the straight path and goes in a crooked way.

My son, the stumbling of a man with his foot is better than the stumbling of a man with his tongue.

My son, a friend who is near is better than a more excellent brother who is far away.

My son, beauty fades but learning lasts, and the world fades and becomes vain, but a good name neither becomes vain nor fades.

My son, for the man who has no peace, his death is better than his life, and the sound of mourning is better than the sound of singing. If the fear of God is in them, sorrow and weeping are better than the sound of singing and rejoicing.

My child, the leg of a frog in your hand is better than a goose in the pot of your neighbor, and a sheep near you is better than an ox far away, and a sparrow in your hand is better than a thousand sparrows flying. Poverty which gathers is better than the scattering of many provisions, and a living fox is better than a dead lion. A pound of wool is better than a pound of gold or silver, for the gold and the silver are hidden and covered up in the earth and are not seen, but the wool stays in the markets and it is seen, and it is a beauty to him who wears it.

My son, a small fortune is better than a scattered fortune.

My son, a living dog is better than a dead poor man.

My son, a poor man who does right is better than a rich man who is dead because of his sins.

My son, keep a word in your heart, and it will be much to you and beware that you don't reveal the secret of your friend.

My son, don't let a word issue from your mouth until you have taken counsel with your heart. Stand not between quarreling people, because from an insult there comes a quarrel, and from a quarrel there comes a dispute, and from dispute there comes fighting, and you will be forced to bear witness. Instead, run from there and have peace.

My son, don't struggle with a man stronger than yourself, but have a patient spirit, and endure in upright conduct, for there is nothing more excellent than that.

My son, don't hate your first friend, for the second one may not last.

My son, visit the poor in his affliction, and speak of him in the king's presence, and do your diligence to save him from the mouth of the lion.

My son, don't rejoice in the death of your enemy, for after a little while you will be his neighbor, and he who mocks you, you respect and honor and greeting him first.

My son, if water would stand still in the sky, and a black crow become white, and myrrh grows sweet as honey, then ignorant men and fools might understand and become wise.

My son, if you desire to be wise, restrain your tongue from lying, and your hand from stealing, and your eyes from seeing evil, and then you will be called wise.

My son, let the wise man beat you with a wand but don't let the fool anoint you with sweet salve. Be humble in your youth and you will be honored in your old age.

My son, don't stand against a man in the days of his power, or a river in the days of its flood.

My son, do not rush to wed a wife, for if it turns out well, she will say, "My lord, make provision for me," and if it turns out poorly, she will accuse him who was the cause of it.

My son, whoever is elegant in his dress, he is the same in his speech, and he who has a mean appearance in his dress, he also is the same in his speech.

My son, if you have committed a theft, make it known to the king, and give him a share of it, that you may be delivered from him, for otherwise, you will endure bitterness.

My son, make a friend of the man whose hand is satisfied and filled and don't make friends with the man whose hand is closed and hungry.

There are four things in which neither the king nor his army can be secure: oppression by the vizier, bad government, perversion of the will, and tyranny over the subjects, and four things which cannot be hidden: the prudent, the foolish, the rich, and the poor."

Ahihar Restoration: Chapter 2 Notes

1) Aramaic: Bôlå (𐡀𐡋𐡏𐡁). Translation: Bel (or Ba'al, Lord)

• Greek: Cyrios (Κύριος). Translation: lord

• Armenian: Ter (Sȶp). Translation: owner (or lord, master)

• Arabic: āllh (الله). Translation: god

• Old Slavonic: Gospodĭ (Ⰳⱁⱄⱂⱁⰴⱐ). Translation: lord (or master)

The various later translations indicate that the Christian and/or Islamic God is being referred to, however, scholars believe the Aramaic version was referring to Bel, the supreme god of the Neo-Babylonian pantheon. If this analysis is correct, it means the Neo-Assyrian Cuneiform text of Ahikar must have been translated into Aramaic in the Neo-Babylonian Empire, which supports the removal of the name of Ashurbanipal. Bel was worshiped by the Babylonians in the first millennium BC. He was a syncretization of the older Mesopotamian Marduk, Enlil, and Dumuzid. However, his name simply translates as 'Lord,' meaning that Ahikar could have simply been using the term 'Lord.'

Whichever god Ahikar was referring to, if he was living in Assyria under Ashurbanipal, he would not have been worshiping the god of the renegade Neo-Babylonians, meaning that Bel can only be accepted as the original god in the text if it is assumed that Ahikar did not exist, and the book is a work of fiction, written in the Neo-Babylonian era. However, this also seems improbable, as a book about a Samaritan worshiper of Bel living in the Neo-Assyrian Empire, should anyone decide to write something so obscure, would have been written in Neo-Babylonian Cuneiform, and probably not translated into Aramaic until the Persian era, resulting in the reading of 'Bel' being erased by the Israelites abandoning the title Ba'al for their god during the Neo-Babylonian era in response

Bel being the supreme god of the people who destroyed Jerusalem. As the setting of the book is Assyria, not Babylonia, the Assyrian reading of Belu (-𒂗) is used in this translation, generally rendering the term as 'Lord,' as it appears in Greek, Aramaic, and Old Slavonic translations.

There are specific references to an Idol of Bel/Lord/Allah, however, as there was no known statue at the time of the Lord or Allah, the translation of Bel is used, however, it is unlikely Bel was originally in the Neo-Assyrian text. The references to the Idol of Bel, take place in 'Egypt,' which may have been Kush at the time when Ahikar was speaking to the Pharaoh, indicating that the author was referring to an Egyptian or Kushite god, not a Babylonian god. As the name of the god is no longer in any of the texts, the reference to Bel is used in relation to the idol.

2) Colocynth, also called bitter apples, is a viny plant native to the Mediterranean region and was once cultivated across Anatolia, the Middle East, Egypt, and Kush. It was cultivated in Egypt since pre-Dynastic times, since at least 3800 BC. By the classical era, it was mainly used for medicine. Today it is primarily cultivated for medicine or bio-fuel.

Ahihar Restoration: Chapter 3

So spoke Ahikar, and when he had finished these injunctions and proverbs to Nadan, his sister's son, he imagined that he would keep them all, and he did not know that instead, that he was seeing him as weary and contemptible, and mocking him. Ahikar sat in his house afterward and gave to Nadan all his goods, and the slaves, and the handmaidens, and the horses, and the livestock, and everything else that he had possessed and gained, and the power of bidding and of forbidding was given to the hand of Nadan. Ahikar sat in peace in his house, and occasionally Ahikar went and paid his respects to the king, and returned home.

When Nadan saw that the power of bidding and forbidding was in his hands, he despised the position of Ahikar and scoffed at him, and set about blaming him whenever he appeared, saying, "My uncle Ahikar is in his old age, and he knows nothing anymore."

He began to beat the slaves and the handmaidens and to sell the horses and the camels and he spent all that his uncle Ahikar had owned. When Ahikar saw that he had no compassion on his servants or his household, he arose and chased him from his house, and sent a message to inform the king that he had scattered his possessions and his provision.

The king arose and called Nadan and said to him, "While Ahikar remains in health, no one will rule his goods, or his household, or over his possessions."

The hand of Nadan was lifted off from his uncle Ahikar and all his goods, and in the meantime, he neither went in or out nor did he greet him. Afterward, Ahikar regretted the struggle with Nadan his sister's son, and he continued to be very sad. Nadan had a younger brother named Benuzardan, so Ahikar took him for himself instead of Nadan, and raised him and honored him with the greatest honors. He gave over to him all that he possessed and made him ruler of his house.

Now when Nadan found out what had happened he was seized with envy and jealousy, and he began to complain to everyone who questioned him, and to mock his, uncle Ahikar, saying, "My uncle has chased me from his house and has preferred my brother to me, but if the Highest God gives me the power, I will cause him to be killed."

Nadan thought about what trap he might set for him. After a while, Nadan turned it over in his mind and wrote a letter to Bel-Iqisha,[1] servant of King Teumman,[2] the king of Elam,[3] saying:

> "Peace and health and strength and honor from Ashur-banipal, king of Nineveh in Assyria, and from his vizier and

his secretary Ahikar to you, great king! Let there be peace between you and me.

When this letter reaches you, if you will rise and go quickly to the plains of the protectors,[4] and to Nineveh in Assyria, I will deliver up the kingdom to you without war and without a battle-formation."

He wrote also another letter in the name of Ahikar to Pharaoh king of Egypt:[5]

"Let there be peace between you and me, mighty king!

If at the time when this letter reaches you, you rise and go to Nineveh in Assyria to the plain of the protectors, I will deliver up to you the kingdom without war and without fighting."

The letters of Nadan looked like the letters of his uncle Ahikar. He folded the two letters and sealed them with the seal of his uncle Ahikar, and they were left in the king's palace. Then he went and wrote a similar letter from the king to his uncle Ahikar:

"Peace and health to my vizier, my secretary, my chancellor, Ahikar,

Ahikar, when this letter reaches you, assemble all the soldiers who are with you, and let them be in perfect clothing and in great numbers, and bring them to me on the fifth day in the plain of the protectors.

When you see me there coming towards you, quickly have the army move against me like an enemy who would

fight with me, for I have with me the ambassadors of
Pharaoh king of Egypt, that they may see the strength of
our army and may fear us, for they are our enemies and
they hate us."

Then he sealed the letter and sent it to Ahikar by one
of the king's servants. He took the other letter which he
had written and spread it before the king and read it to
him and showed him the seal. When the king heard
what was in the letter he was perplexed and greatly
confused and fiercely angry, and said, "Oh, I have been
shown wisdom! What have I done to Ahikar that he has
written these letters to my enemies? Is this my repayment for my gifts to him?"

Nadan said to him, "Do not be sad, king! Nor be angry,
but let us go to the plain of the protectors and see if the
story is true or not."

Then Nadan arose on the fifth day and took the king
and the soldiers and the vizier, and they went to the
desert to the plain of the protectors. The king looked and
saw Ahikar and the army set in formation. When
Ahikar saw that the king was there, he approached and
signaled to the army to move as they would in war and
to fight in formation against the king as it had been told
in the letter, not knowing the trap Nadan had set for
him.

When the king saw the acts of Ahikar he was seized with anxiety and terror and confusion and was very angry. Nadan said to him, "Have you seen, my lord the king, what this wretch has done? Do not be angry and do not be sad or hurt, but go to your house and sit on your throne, and I will bring Ahikar to you bound and chained with chains, and I will chase away your enemy from before you without a battle."

The king returned to his throne, being provoked about Ahikar, and did nothing about him. Nadan went to Ahikar and said to him, "Hello, my uncle! The king is very happy with you, and thanks you for having done what he commanded you. Now he has sent me to you that you may dismiss the soldiers to their duties and come yourself to him with your hands bound behind you, and your feet chained, that the ambassadors of Pharaoh may see this and that the king may be feared by them and by their king."

Then Ahikar answered, "To hear is to obey."

He arose right away and bound his hands behind him, and chained his feet, and Nadan took him to the king. When Ahikar entered the king's presence he did obeisance before him on the ground and wished for power and perpetual life to the king. Then the king demanded, "Ahikar, my secretary, the governor of my affairs, my chancellor, the ruler of my state, tell me what evil have

I done to you that you have rewarded me by this terrible deed."

Then they showed him the letters in his writing and with his seal. When Ahikar saw this, his limbs trembled and his tongue was tied at once, and he was unable to speak a word from fear, but he hung his head towards the earth and was dumb. When the king saw this, he felt certain that the scheme was from him, and he immediately rose and commanded them to execute Ahikar and to chop his neck with the sword outside of the city. Then Nadan screamed and said, "Ahikar! What makes you thing you can do things to the king?"

(So says the story-teller.)

The name of the swordsman was Abi Samik. The king said to him, "Swordsman! Rise and go cut the neck of Ahikar at the door of his house, and throw away his head from his body a hundred cubits."

Then Ahikar knelt before the king, and said, "Let my lord the king live forever! If you desire to slay me, let your wish be fulfilled, and I know that I am not guilty, but the wicked man has to give an account of his wickedness, nevertheless, my lord the king, I beg of you and from your friendship, permit the swordsman to give my body to my slaves, that they may bury me, and let your slave be your sacrifice."

The king rose and commanded the swordsman to do with him according to his desire. He immediately commanded his servants to take Ahikar and the swordsman and take him naked, so they might slay him. When Ahikar knew for certain that he was to be slain he sent a message to his wife, and said to her, "Come out and meet me, and let there be with you a thousand young virgins, and dress them in gowns of purple and silk that they may cry for me before my death. Prepare a table for the swordsman and his servants, and prepare plenty of wine, that they may drink."

She did all that he commanded her. She was very wise, clever, and prudent. She united all possible courtesy and learning. When the army of the king and the swordsman arrived, he found the table set in order, and the wine and the luxurious viands, and they began eating and drinking till they were gorged and drunken.

Then Ahikar took the swordsman aside, separate from the company and said, "Abi Samik, do you not know that when Esarhaddon the king, the father of Ashurbanipal, wanted to kill you, I took you and hid you in a certain place until the king's anger subsided and he asked for you?"

"When I brought you into his presence he rejoiced in you, and now remember the kindness I did you. I know that the king will be sorry about me and will be very angry about my execution. For I am not guilty, and it will happen when you present me before him in his palace, you will meet with great fortune, and know that Nadan my sister's son has deceived me and has done this terrible deed to me, and the king will repent of having killed me. I have a well in the garden of my house, and no one knows of it. Hide me in it with only my wife knowing. I have a slave in prison who deserves to be killed. Bring him out and dress him in my clothes, and command the servants when they are drunk to slay him. They will not know who it is they are killing. Throw away his head a hundred cubits from his body, and give his body to my slaves that they may bury it. You have laid up a great treasure with me."

Then the swordsman did as Ahikar had commanded him, and he went to the king and said to him, "May you live forever!"

Then each week, Ahikar's wife lowered down to him in his hiding-place everything he needed, and no one else knew of it. The story was reported and repeated and spread abroad in every place of how Ahikar the Sage had been slain and was dead, and all the people of that city mourned for him. They wept and said, "Alas for you, Ahikar, and for your learning and your courtesy! How sad it is to lose you and your knowledge! Where can another like you be found? Where can there be a man so intelligent, learned, and skilled in ruling as to resemble you that he may fill your place?"

The king repented killing Ahikar, but his repentance did not help him. Then he called for Nadan and said to him, "Go, and take your friends with you, and mourn and cry for your uncle Ahikar, and lament for him as is the custom, honoring in his memory."

But when Nadan, the foolish, the ignorant, the hard-hearted, went to the house of his uncle, he neither wept nor mourned nor wailed, but assembled heartless and dissolute people and set about eating and drinking. Nadan began to seize the woman-slaves and the men-slaves belonging to Ahikar, and bound them and tortured them and beat them severely. He did not respect the wife of his uncle, she who had brought him up like her own son, but wanted her to sin with him. Ahikar had been in the hiding-place, and he heard the weeping of his slaves and his neighbors, and he praised the Highest God, the Merciful One, and gave thanks, and he continued to pray and implore the Highest God.

The swordsman came from time to time to Ahikar while he was in the hiding-place, and Ahikar came and begged him. He comforted him and wished him deliverance. When the story was reported in other countries that Ahikar the Sage had been murdered, all the kings were sad and hated king Ashurbanipal, and they lamented over Ahikar the solver of riddles.

Ahihar Restoration: Chapter 3 Notes

1) Aramaic: Ȧkiš (ʋ^ɥN)

- Greek: Acchous (Ακχους)

- Armenian: Akhis (Ա.խիհu)

- Arabic: Ȧḫyš (أخيش)

While the text refers to this as the son of 'King Wise of Persia,' it is likely that this began as a reference the Aramean chieftain Bel-Iqisha, who led an Elamite backed rebellion in southern Babylonian in 665 BC. Ȧkiš (ʷⱿᎽ¥) was also a popular Canaanite name at the time, and several Philistine kings bore the name, which was recorded in Neo-Assyrian Cuneiform as Ikaúsu (𒀸𒋗𒌋𒐋𒋤).

2) All translations refer to a 'King Wise, however, there are no records of any Persian king named any variation of the word 'wise,' and at Persia did not exist as a kingdom at the time, this was probably a mistranslation of the name of the Elamite king Teumman, who backed the rebellion of Bel-Iqisha in 664 BC. Teumman's name was virtually the same as the Babylonian word tēmānu (𒁹𒌋), which meant 'wise,' suggesting that the original Neo-Assyrian story was about King Teumman and his proxy Bel-Iqisha.

3) All translations that survive to the present refer to this land as Persia, however, the Book of Tobit refers to it as Elam. This suggests that the term Persia was used in the original Aramaic translation made in the Neo-Babylonian Empire, which appears to have served for all later translations. This is historically valid, as Persia became a kingdom during the Neo-Babylonian era, and Elam

no longer existed by the time that Babylon and its allies overthrew Assyria.

4) The word Nisrin, appear to be a Persian reinterpretation of the older Neo-Assyrian cuneiform word naṣārum (𒈨𒃶𒌋). The Persian word nasrin (نسرین) means roses, while the Akkadian word meant 'protectors.' As the described geography places the Plain of Roses/Protectors in the region around Nineveh, and the Assyrians spoke Assyrian, and not Persian, the original meaning is restored.

5) All translations agree that this was Egypt, which if the previous references were to Bel-Iqisha and King Teumman in 664 BC, would make this the first regal year of Pharaoh Wahibre Psamtik I, however, at the beginning of his reign he did not control Egypt, as the Kushites had invaded and captured most of the country, and in the process killed his predecessor Pharaoh Necho I. If Nadan had sent a letter to the king of Egypt at the time it would have been King Tantamani of Kush, who was at war against Assyria. The following year, 663 BC, the Assyrian army reinvaded Egypt and drove out the Kushites, and spent the next few years occupying southern Egypt, meaning it could not have been later than 664 BC.

Ahihar Restoration: Chapter 4

When the king of Egypt[1] had heard that Ahikar was dead, he rose immediately and wrote a letter to King Ashurbanipal, saying:

"Peace, health, might, and honor which we wish especially for you, my beloved brother, king Ashurbanipal.

I have been desiring to build a castle in the air between the sky and the earth, and I want you to send me a wise, clever man from yourself to build it for me, and to answer me all my questions, and that I may have the tribute and the custom duties of Assyria for three years."

Then he sealed the letter and sent it to Ashurbanipal, who took it and read it and gave it to his viziers and to the nobles of his kingdom, and they were confused and ashamed. He was very angry and was puzzled about how he should act. Then he assembled the old men and the learned men and the wise men and the philosophers, and the diviners and the astrologers, and everyone who was in his country, and read them the letter and said to them, "Who among you will go to Pharaoh king of Egypt and answer his riddles?"

They answered him, "Our lord king, you know that there is none in your kingdom who is acquainted with these riddles except Ahikar, your vizier and secretary. But as for us, we have no skill in this, unless it is Nadan, his sister's son, for he taught him all his wisdom and learning and knowledge. Call him to you, maybe he may untie this difficult knot."

Then the king called Nadan and said to him, "Look at this letter and understand what is in it."

When Nadan read it, he said, "My lord, who is able to build a castle in the air between the sky and the earth?"

When the king heard the question of Nadan he was very sad, and climbed down from his throne and sat in the ashes, and began to cry and wail over Ahikar saying, "My grief! Ahikar, who knew the secrets and the riddles! Woe to me, Ahikar! Teacher of my country and ruler of my kingdom, where will I find another like you? Ahikar, teacher of my country, where will I turn for you? Woe to me over you! How could I destroy you, and I listened to the talk of a stupid, ignorant boy without knowledge, without religion, without manliness. Why, and why again? Who can give you to me just for once, or bring me word that Ahikar is alive? I would give him half of my kingdom! What is this to me? Oh, Ahikar! That I might see you just once more. Oh! My grief for you, for all time! Ahikar, why have I killed you, and did not delay your case until I had seen all the information?"

The king went on weeping night and day, and when the swordsman saw the anger of the king and his sorrow for Ahikar, his heart was softened towards him, and he entered into his presence and said to him, "My lord! Command your servants to cut off my head."

Then the king asked him, "Why Abi Samik, what is your fault?"

The swordsman said to him, "My master! Every slave who acts contrary to the word of his master is killed, and I have acted contrary to your command."

Then the king asked him, "Why Abi Samik? In what way have you disobeyed my command?"

The swordsman answered him, "My lord! You commanded me to kill Ahikar, and I knew that you would have regret concerning him and that he had been wronged, and I hid him in a certain place, and I killed one of his slaves, and he is now safe in the well, and if you command me I will bring him to you."

The king said to him, "Shame on you, Abi Samik! You are mocking me and I am your lord."

The swordsman replied to him, "No, but by your life, my lord! Ahikar is safe and alive."

When the king heard this, he felt sure of the matter, and his head swam, and he fainted from joy. He commanded them to bring Ahikar. He said to the swordsman, "Trusty servant! If your words are true, I will greatly enrich you, and praise you above all your friends."

The swordsman went out rejoicing and traveled to Ahikar's house. He opened the door of the hiding-place, and went down and found Ahikar sitting, praising God, and thanking him. He called to him, saying, "Ahikar, I bring the greatest of joy, and happiness, and delight!"

Ahikar asked him, "What is the news, Abi Samik?"

He told him all about Pharaoh from the beginning to the end. Then he took him and went to the king. When the king looked at him, he saw him in a state of need, and that his hair had grown long like the wild beasts' and his nails were like the claws of an eagle, and that his body was dirty with dust, and the color of his face had changed and faded and was now like ashes. When the king saw him he was sad because of him and rose at once and embraced him and kissed him, and wept over him and said, "Praise the god who has brought you back to me."

Then he consoled him and comforted him. He stripped off his robe, and put it on the swordsman, and was very gracious to him, and gave him great wealth, and gave Ahikar peace. Then Ahikar said to the king, "Let my lord the king live forever! These are the deeds of the children of the world. I have raised a palm-tree that I might lean on it, and it bent sideways and threw me down. My lord, since I have appeared before you, don't let concerns oppress you!"

The king said to him, "Blessed is the god, who showed you mercy, and knew that you were wronged, and saved you and delivered you from being slain. Go to the warm bath, and shave your head, and cut your nails, and change your clothes, and amuse yourself for forty days, that you may be good to yourself and improve your condition and the color of your face may come back to you."

Then the king stripped off his costly robe and put it on Ahikar, and Ahikar thanked God and did obeisance to the king, and departed to his house glad and happy, praising the Highest God. The people of his household rejoiced with him, and his friends and everyone who heard that he was alive rejoiced also.

Ahihar Restoration: Chapter 4 Notes

1) Assuming that the original Assyrian king in the story was Ashurbanipal, then this would have to be King Psamtik I, who ruled Egypt from 663 BC, when Ashurbanipal placed him on the throne of Egypt as an Assyrian vassal to 610 BC, several decades after the fall of Assyria. There are no surviving records of him attempting to build a castle in the sky, or anything else of significance. Most of his reign seems to have been focused on military campaigns and politics. He managed to defend Egypt from any further Kushite incursions, and successfully transitioned the country from being an Assyrian vassal to an independent nation. After Assyria fell, he spent the next few couple of decades competing with the Babylonians for control of Canaan.

Ahihar Restoration: Chapter 5

He did as the king commanded him, and rested for forty days. Then he dressed himself in his nicest clothes, and rode to the king, with his slaves behind him and before him, rejoicing and delighted. But when Nadan saw what was happening, fear took hold of him and terror, and he was confused, not knowing what to do. When Ahikar saw it he entered into the king's presence and greeted him, and he returned the greeting, and made him sit down at his side, saying to him, "My friend Ahikar! Look at these letters which the king of Egypt sent to us after he heard that you were killed. They have provoked us and confused us, and many of the people of our country have fled to Egypt in fear of the tribute that the king of Egypt has demanded from us."

Then Ahikar took the letter and read it, and understood its contents. Then he said to the king, "Do not be angry, my lord! I will go to Egypt, and I will return the answers to Pharaoh, and I will display this letter to him, and I will reply to him about the tribute, and I will send back all those who have run away, and I will put your enemies to shame with the help of the Highest God, and for the happiness of your kingdom."

When the king heard this speech from Ahikar he rejoiced greatly, and his heart was expanded and he showed him favor. Ahikar asked the king, "Grant me a delay of forty days that I may consider this question and answer it."

The king permitted this, and Ahikar returned to his home. He commanded the hunters to capture two young eagles for him, and they captured them and brought them to him. He commanded the weavers of ropes to weave two cotton ropes for him, each two thousand cubits long. He had the carpenters brought to him and ordered them to make two great boxes, which they did. Then he took two young boys, and spent every day sacrificing lambs, and feeding the eagles and the boys. He made the boys ride on the backs of the eagles, and he bound them with a firm knot, and tied the cable to the feet of the eagles, and let them soar upwards little by little every day, to a distance of ten cubits, until they grew used to it and were trained to do it. They rose all the length of the rope until they reached the sky, with the boys on their backs. Then he pulled them back to himself.

When Ahikar saw that his plan was working he ordered the boys that when they were carried up into the sky, they were to shout, "Bring us clay and stone, so we can build a castle for king Pharaoh, as we are idle."

Ahikar was never done training them and exercising them until they had reached the highest possible place.

Then leaving them he went to the king and said to him, "My lord! The work is finished as to your desire. Rise with me that I may show you the wonder."

So the king got up and sat with Ahikar and went to a wide place and sent to bring the eagles and the boys, and Ahikar tied them and let them up into the air all the length of the ropes, and they began to shout as he had taught them. Then he drew them to himself and put them in their places. The king and those who were with him wondered greatly, and the king kissed Ahikar between his eyes and said to him, "Go in peace, my friend, pride of my kingdom, to Egypt and answer the riddles of Pharaoh and overcome him by the strength of the Highest God."

Then he commanded him farewell, and took his troops and his army and the young men and the eagles, and went towards the dwellings of Egypt, and when he had arrived, he turned towards the country of the king.

When the people of Egypt knew that Ashurbanipal had sent a man of his trusted council to talk with Pharaoh and to answer his questions, they took the news to king Pharaoh, and he sent a party of his trusted councilors to bring him before him.

He came and entered into the presence of Pharaoh, and did obeisance to him as it is fitting to do to kings, and he said to him, "My lord the king, Ashurbanipal the king hails you with abundance of peace and might, and honor. He has sent me, who is one of his servants, that I may answer you your questions, and may fulfill all your desire, for you have sent a message to my lord the king seeking a man who will build you a castle between the sky and the earth. I, through the help of the Highest God and your noble favor and the power of my lord the king will build it for you as you desire. But, my lord king, what you have said about the tribute of Egypt for three years, now the stability of a kingdom is strict justice, and if you win and my hand has no skill in replying to you, then my lord the king will send you the tribute which you have mentioned. If I will have answered you in your questions, it will remain for you to send whatever you have mentioned to my lord the king."

When Pharaoh heard that speech, he wondered and was perplexed by the freedom of his tongue and the pleasantness of his speech. King Pharaoh asked him, "Man, what is your name?"

He answered, "Your servant is Abi Qam, and I am but a little ant among the ants of King Ashurbanipal."

Pharaoh said to him, "Has your lord no one of higher dignity than you, that he has sent me a little ant to reply to me, and to talk with me?"

Ahikar said to him, "My lord king! I will pray to God Highest that I may fulfill what is on your mind, for God is with the weak that he may confound the strong."

Then Pharaoh commanded that they should prepare a living place for Abi Qam and supply him with provisions, meat, and drink, and all that he needed. When it was finished, three days afterward Pharaoh clothed himself in purple and red and sat on his throne, and all his viziers and the magnates of his kingdom were standing with their hands crossed, their feet close together, and their heads bowed.

Pharaoh sent to fetch Abi Qam, and when he was presented to him, he did obeisance before him, and kissed the ground in front of him. King Pharaoh asked him, "Abi Qam, who am I like? And the nobles of my kingdom, who are they like?"

Ahikar answered him, "My lord king, you are like the god Bel, and the nobles of your kingdom are like his servants."

He said to him, "Go, and come back here tomorrow."

So Ahikar left as king Pharaoh had commanded him. In the morning, Ahikar returned into the presence of Pharaoh, and did obeisance, and stood before the king. Pharaoh was dressed in a red, and the nobles were dressed in white. Pharaoh asked him, "Abi Qam, who am

I like? And the nobles of my kingdom, who are they like?"

Ahikar answered him, "My lord, you are like the sun, and your servants are like its beams."

Pharaoh replied to him, "Go to your home, and return here tomorrow."

Then Pharaoh commanded his court to wear pure white, and Pharaoh was dressed like them and sat on his throne, and he commanded them to fetch Ahikar. He entered and sat down before him, and Pharaoh asked him, "Abi Qam, who am I like? And my nobles, who are they like?"

Abi Qam answered him, "My lord, you are like the moon, and your nobles are like the planets and the stars."

Pharaoh replied to him, "Go, and tomorrow return here."

Then Pharaoh commanded his servants to wear robes of various colors, and Pharaoh wore a red velvet dress, and sat on his throne, and commanded them to bring in Abi Qam. He entered and did obeisance before him, and he asked, "Abi Qam, who am I like? And my armies, who are they like?"

He answered, "My lord, you are like the month of Parmouti,[1] and your armies are like its flowers."

When the king heard it he rejoiced greatly and said, "The first time you compared me to the idol Bel, and my nobles to his servants. The second time you compared me to the sun, and my nobles to the sunbeams. The third time you compared me to the moon, and my nobles to the planets and the stars. The fourth time you compared me to the month of Parmouti, and my nobles to its flowers. But now, Abi Qam, tell me, your lord King Ashurbanipal, who is he like? And his nobles, who are they like?"

Ahikar shouted with a loud voice and said, "It is far from me to make mention of my lord the king, while you are seated on your throne. Get up on your feet that I may tell you who my lord the king is like and who his nobles are like."

Pharaoh was confused by the freedom of his words and his boldness in answering. Pharaoh rose from his throne, and stood before Ahikar, and said, "Tell me now, that I may know who your lord the king is like, and who his nobles are like."

Ahikar said to him, "My lord is the sky god, and his nobles are the lightning and the thunder, and when he wills it, the winds blow and the rain falls. He commands the thunder, and there is lightning and rain, and he holds the Sun, and it does not give its light, and the moon and the stars, and they don't circle. He commands the tempest, and it blows and the rain falls and it tramples in Parmouti and destroys its flowers and its houses."

When Pharaoh heard this speech, he was very confused and was extremely angry, and said to him, "Man, tell me the truth, and let me know who you really are."

He admitted the truth, "I am Ahikar the scribe, greatest of the trusted councilors of King Ashurbanipal, and I am his vizier and the governor of his kingdom, and his chancellor."

He said to him, "You have told the truth in this saying. But we have heard that king Ashurbanipal has executed Ahikar, yet you seem to be alive and well."

Ahikar answered him, "Yes, so it was, but praise be to God, who knows what is hidden, for my lord the king commanded me to be killed, and he believed the lies told of men, but the Lord saved me, and blessed is he who trusts in him."

Pharaoh said to Ahikar, "Go, and tomorrow return here, and tell me something that I have never heard from my nobles or the people of my kingdom and my country."

Ahihar Restoration: Chapter 5 Notes

1) Greek: Pharmouthi (Φαρμουθί)

- Armenian: Pôarmutôi (Փարմութի)

- Arabic: Baramūdah (برمودة)

Pȧ-en-renen-wetet (𓉐 𓈖 𓏏 𓂧 𓆄) was the eight month of the Egyptian civil calendar, and the last month of the Season of the Emergence (𓈉 𓇳), when the Nile floods receded and the crops started to grow. It continued into the Coptic calendars as Parmouti (Παρμογτε) and Tharmouthi (Φαρμογϯ). This month is approximately April 9 to May 8 on the Gregorian calendar during the 21st-century. It is generally translated as Parmouti in English from the Sahidic dialect of Coptic.

Ahihar Restoration: Chapter 6

Ahikar returned to his residence, and wrote a letter, saying in it on this:

"From King Ashurbanipal of Nineveh in Assyria to Pharaoh king of Egypt.

Peace be on you, my brother!

Let us make known to you through this message that a brother needs his brother, and kings of each other, and my hope from you is that you would lend me nine hundred talents of gold, for I need it for the provisioning of some of the soldiers, and I will spend it on them. At some point, I will return it to you."

Then he folded the letter and presented it in the morning to Pharaoh. When he saw it, he was confused and said to him, "I have never heard anything like these words from anyone."

Then Ahikar said to him, "Truly this is a debt which you owe to my lord the king."

Pharaoh accepted this, saying, "Ahikar, it is your way to be honest in the service of kings. Blessed be God who has made you perfect in wisdom and has adorned you with philosophy and knowledge. Now, Ahikar, there remains what we desire from you, that you should build as a castle between the sky and earth."

Then Ahikar replied, "To hear is to obey. I will build you a castle as you wish, but, my lord I will need lime, stone, clay, and workmen prepared. I have skilled builders who will build it for you as you desire."

The king prepared everything for him, and they went to a wide place where Ahikar also came, and he took the eagles and the young boys with him. The king and all his nobles went and the whole city assembled, that they might see what Ahikar would do. Then Ahikar let the eagles out of the boxes, and tied the young men on their backs, and tied the ropes to the eagles' feet, and let them go in the air. They soared upwards, till they were between the sky and earth.

The boys began to shout, saying, "Bring bricks, bring clay, that we may build the king's castle, for we are standing idle!"

The crowd was astonished and perplexed, and they wondered. The king and his nobles wondered. Ahikar and his servants began to beat the workmen, and they shouted for the king's troops, saying to them, "Bring the skilled workmen what they want and do not stop them from their work."

The king said to him, "You are mad, who can bring anything up to that height?"

Ahikar said to him, "My lord, how will we build a castle in the air? If my lord the king were here, he would have built several castles in a single day."

Pharaoh said to him, "Leave Ahikar, to your residence, and rest. We have given up building the castle, but tomorrow return to me."

Then Ahikar went to his residence and in the morning he returned to Pharaoh, and Pharaoh said, "Ahikar, what news is there of the horse of your lord? When he neighs in Nineveh in the country of Assyria, and our mares hear his voice, they abandon their young."

When Ahikar heard this riddle he went and took a cat, and tied her up and began to flog her violently until the Egyptians heard it, and they went and told the king about it. Pharaoh sent for Ahikar, and said to him, "Ahikar, why do you flog and beat that dumb animal?"

Ahikar said to him, my lord the king, she has done an ugly deed to me and has deserved this beating and flogging, for my lord King Ashurbanipal had given me a fine rooster, and he had a strong true voice and knew the hours of the day and the night. The cat got up this very night and bit off its head and went away, and because of this deed I have beaten her."

Pharaoh said to him, "Ahikar, I see from all this that you are growing old and are losing your mind, for between Egypt and Nineveh there are sixty-eight iterus,[1] and how did she go this very night and cut off the head of your rooster and returned?"

Ahikar said to him, "My lord, if there is such a distance between Egypt and Nineveh how could your mares hear when my lord the king's horse neighs and abandon their young? How could the voice of the horse reach Egypt?"

When Pharaoh heard that, he knew that Ahikar had answered his riddle, and Pharaoh said, "Ahikar, I want you to make me ropes from the sea-sand."

Ahikar said to him, "My lord king, order them to bring me a rope out of the treasury that I may make one like it."

Then Ahikar went to the back of the house, and drilled holes in the rough shape of the sea, and took a handful of sand in his hand, sea-sand. When the sun rose and shone through the holes, he spread the sand in the sun till it looked like woven like ropes. Ahikar said, "Command your servants to take these ropes, and whenever you desire it, I will weave you some more like them."

Pharaoh said, "Ahikar, we have a millstone here and it has been broken and I want you to sew it up."

Then Ahikar looked at it and found another stone. He said, "My lord, I am a foreigner, and I have no tool for sewing. But I want you to command your faithful shoe-makers to cut awls from this stone, that I may sew that millstone."

Then Pharaoh and all his nobles laughed. He said, "Blessed be the Highest God, who gave you this wit and knowledge."

When Pharaoh saw that Ahikar had overcome him, and answered his riddles, he at once became excited and commanded them to collect for him three years' tribute and to bring them to Ahikar. He stripped off his robes and put them on Ahikar, and his soldiers, and his servants, and gave him the expenses of his journey. He said to him, "Go in peace, strength of your lord and pride of your teachers. Have any of the kingSultans your like? Give my greetings to your lord King Ashurbanipal, and say to him how we have sent him gifts, for kings are content with little."

Then Ahikar arose, and kissed king Pharaoh's hands and kissed the ground in front of him, and wished him strength and continuance, and abundance in his treasury, and said to him, "My lord, I desire from you that not one of our countrymen may remain in Egypt."

Pharaoh rose and sent heralds to proclaim in the streets of Egypt that not one of the people of Nineveh in Assyria should remain in the land of Egypt, but that they should go with Ahikar. Then Ahikar left King

Pharaoh and traveled to Nineveh in the land of Assyria and he had some treasures and a great deal of wealth.

When the news reached King Ashurbanipal that Ahikar was coming, he went out to meet him and rejoiced over him exceedingly with great joy and embraced him and kissed him and said to him, "Welcome home, my relative, my brother Ahikar, the strength of my kingdom, and pride of my realm. Ask what you would have from me, even if you desire half of my kingdom and my possessions."

Then Ahikar said to him, "My lord king, live forever! Show favor, my lord king, to Abi Samik instead of me, for my life was in the hands of God and also his."

Then King Ashurbanipal said, "Honor be to you, my beloved Ahikar! I will make the station of Abi Samik the swordsman, higher than all my trusted councilors and my favorites."

Then the king began to ask him how he had dealt with Pharaoh from when he arrived until he had left his presence, and how he had answered all his questions, and how he had received the tribute from him, and the changes of clothing and the presents. King Ashurbanipal celebrated with great joy, and said to Ahikar, "Take what you would have of this tribute, for it is all within your hands."

Ahikar replied, "Let the king live forever! I desire nothing but the safety of my lord king and the continuance of his greatness. My lord, what can I do with wealth and its like? But if you will show me favor, give me Nadan, my sister's son, that I may repay him for what he has done to me, and grant me his blood and hold me guiltless of it."

Ashurbanipal the king said, "Take him, I have given him to you."

Ahikar took Nadan, his sister's son, and bound his hands with chains of iron, and took him to his home, and put heavy shackles on his feet, and tied it with a tight knot, and after binding him so he threw him into a dark room, beside the retiring-place, and appointed Nebu-hal as watchman over him to give him a loaf of bread and a little water every day.

Ahihar Restoration: Chapter 6 Notes

1) Aramaic: prśhǎ (ℵ𝕽𝕐𝕐𝕻). Translation: parasang (or league)

- Greek: parasángēs (παρασάγγης). Translation: parasang (or league)

- Armenian: hrasax (հրասախ). Translation: parasang (or league)

- Arabic: farsaḵ (فَرْسَخ). Translation: parasang (or league)

The unit of measurement used in the text was the parasang, a Persian unit that was adopted by many other cultures. The term is accepted as having been adopted by other cultures during the Persian era, meaning it must have been a Persian era replacement for an older term. Its length was not consistent, ranging between 4.8 and 5.6 km (3 to 3½ miles). The term could not have been the original term in the text, as 68 parasangs would have only been about 340 km (200 miles), while the distance from the Egyptian capital of Sais to Nineveh would have been 1500 to 1600 kilometers (900 to 1000 miles), depending on the route taken.

The earlier Mesopotamian unit of measurement which is also translated into English as 'league,' was the bêr (𝌆𝌇), which was approximately 2.7 km (1.7 miles) long, even shorter than the parasang. The text implies that the original unit of measurement that the king of Egypt used, was very long as there were only 68 of them between Egypt and Assyria. The longest Egyptian unit of measurement that appears to have been used at the time was the jtrw (𓇋𓏤𓈖𓊖𓏤), which is translated into English as the 'River-Measure League,' as it was a nautical distance. It was approximately 10.5 km (6.5 miles) long, which would make the distance listed approximately 714 km (444 miles), which is only half the distance from Sais to Nineveh. As the unit of measurement was nautical, and the distance mentioned was approximately the distance from Sais to the Assyrian ports in Lebanon, it is plausible that the original text was referring to the Assyrian Empire, and not the city of Nineveh itself.

Ahihar Restoration: Chapter 7

Whenever Ahikar went in or out, he chastised Nadan, his sister's son, saying, "Nadan, my boy, I have done to you all that is good and kind and you have rewarded me for it, with what is ugly and bad and with murder. My son, it is said in the proverbs, 'He who does not listen with his ears, they will make listen with the scruff of his neck.'"

Nadan asked, "Why are you angry with me?"

Ahikar said to him, "Because I raised you, and taught you, and gave you honor and respect and made you great, and reared you with the best of breeding, and seated you in my place that you might be my heir in the world, and you treated me with killing and repaid me with my ruin. But the Lord knew that I was wronged, and he saved me from the trap which you had set for me, for the Lord heals the broken hearts and hinders the envious and the haughty.

My boy, you have been to me like the scorpion which when it strikes on brass, pierces it.

My boy, you are like the gazelle who was eating the roots of the madder, and it adds to me today, but tomorrow they will tan they hide in my roots.

My boy, you have been like he who saw his comrade naked in the winter, and he took cold water and poured it on him.

My boy, you have been to me like a man who took a stone and threw it up to the sky to stone the Lord with it. The stone did not hit and did not reach high enough, but it became the cause of guilt and sin.

My boy, if you had honored me and respected me and had listened to my words you would have been my heir and would have reigned over my dominions.

My son, know that if the tail of the dog or the pig were ten cubits long it would not approach the worth of the horse's even if it were like silk.

My boy! I thought that you would have been my heir at my death, and you through your envy and your insolence desired to kill me. But the Lord delivered me from your cunning.

My son, you have been to me like a trap which was set up on the dunghill, and there came a sparrow and found the trap set up. The sparrow asked the trap, "Why are you here?"

The trap answered, "I am praying here to God."

The lark also asked it, "What is the piece of wood that you hold?"

The trap replied, "That is a young oak-tree on which I lean at the time of prayer."

The lark asked, "What is that thing in your mouth?"

The trap answered, "That is bread and meat which I carry for all the hungry and the poor who come near to me."

The lark asked, "Now then, may I come forward and eat, as I am hungry?"

The trap answered him, "Come forward."

The lark approached so it might eat, but the trap sprang up and seized the lark by its neck. The lark answered and said to the trap, "If that is your bread for the hungry God will not accept your alms and your kind deeds. If that is your fasting and your prayers, God accepts from you neither your fast or your prayer, and God will not perfect what is good concerning you."

My boy, you have been to me like a lion who made friends with a donkey, and the donkey kept walking before the lion for a time, and one day the lion sprang on the donkey and ate it up.

My boy, you have been to me like a weevil in the wheat, for it does nothing good, but spoils the wheat and eats it.

My boy, you have been like a man who sowed ten measures of wheat, and when it was harvest time, he arose and reaped it, and separated it, and threshed it, and struggled over it to the utmost, and it turned out to be ten measures, and its master said to it, "You lazy thing, you have not grown and you have not shrunk."

My boy, you have been to me like the partridge that had been thrown into the net, and she could not save herself, but she called out to the partridges, that she might get them caught in the net with her.

My son, you have been to me like the cold dog and it went into the potter's house to get warm. When it had gotten warm, it began to bark at them, and they chased it out and beat it, that it might not bite them.

My son, you have been to me like the pig who went into the hot bath with people of quality, and when it came out of the hot bath, it saw a muddy hole and it went down and wallowed in it.

My son, you have been to me like the goat which joined its comrades on their way to the sacrifice, and it was unable to save itself.

My boy, the dog which is not fed through its hunting becomes food for flies.

My son, the hand which does not labor and plow and is greedy and cunning will be cut away from its shoulder.

My son, the eye in which light is not seen, the ravens will pick at it and pluck it out.

My boy, you have been to me like a tree whose branches they were cutting, and it said to them, "If something of me were not in your hands, verily you would be unable to cut me."

My boy, you are like the cat to who they said, "Stop stealing until we make you a chain of gold and feed you with sugar and almonds."

She replied, "I am not forgetful of the craft of my father and my mother."

My son, you have been like the serpent riding on a thorn-bush when he was among a river, and a wolf saw them and said, "Mischief on mischief, and let him who is more mischievous than they direct both of them."

The serpent said to the wolf, "The lambs and the goats and the sheep which you have eaten all your life, will you return them to their fathers and their parents or not?"

The wolf answered, "No."

The serpent said to him, "I think that after myself you are the worst of us."

My boy, I fed you with good food and you did not feed me with dry bread.

My boy, I gave you sugared water to drink and good syrup, and you did not give me water from the well to drink.

My boy, I taught you and raised you, and you dug a hiding-place for me and hid me.

My boy, I brought you up with the best upbringing and trained you like a tall cedar, and you have twisted and bent me.

My boy, it was my hope concerning you that you would build me a fortified castle, that I might be concealed from my enemies in it, and you did become to me like one buried in the depth of the earth, but the Lord took pity on me and delivered me from your cunning.

My boy, I wished you well, and you did reward me with evil and hatefulness, and now I would fain tear from your eyes, and make you food for dogs, and cut out your tongue, and take off your head with the edge of the sword, and repay you for your abominable deeds."

When Nadan heard this speech from his uncle Ahikar, he said, "My uncle! Deal with me according to your knowledge, and forgive my sins, for who is there who has sinned like me, or who is there who forgives like you? Accept me, my uncle! Now I will serve in your house, and groom your horses and sweep up the dung of your livestock, and feed your sheep, for I am wicked and you are righteous. I the guilty and you the forgiving."

Ahikar answered him, "My boy, you are like the tree which was fruitless beside the water, and its master decided to cut it down, and it said to him, 'Move me to another place, and if I do not carry fruit, cut me down.'

Its master said to it, 'You've been beside the water and have not borne fruit, how will you carry fruit when you are in another place?'

My boy, the old age of the eagle is better than the youth of the crow.

My boy, they told the wolf, 'Keep away from the sheep in case their dust should harm you.' The wolf said, 'The dregs of the sheep's milk are good for my eyes.'

My boy, they made the wolf go to a school so he might learn to read and they said to him, 'Say A, B...' He said, 'Lamb, goat...'

My boy, they set the donkey down at the table and he fell and began to roll himself in the dust and one said,

"Let him roll himself, for it is his nature, he will not change."

My boy, the saying has been confirmed which goes, 'If you beget a boy, call him your son, and if you teach a boy, call him your slave.'

My boy, he who does good, will meet with good; and he who does evil will meet with evil, for the Lord repays a man according to the measure of his work.

My boy, what will I say more to you than these sayings? The Lord knows what is hidden, and is acquainted with the mysteries and the secrets. He will repay you and will judge, between me and you, and will repay you according to all your deserve."

When Nadan heard that speech from his uncle Ahikar, he swelled up immediately and became like a blown-out canteen. His limbs swelled and his legs and his feet and his side, and he was torn and his belly burst and his intestines were scattered, and he died. His end was destruction, and he went to the grave. For he who digs a pit for his brother will fall into it, and he who sets up traps will be caught in them.

This is what happened and what we found about the Words of Ahikar. Praise God forever. Amen, and peace.

This chronicle is finished with the help of God, may he be praised! Amen, Amen, Amen.

Septuagint Manuscripts

The following is a list of the Septuagint manuscripts referenced in the notes for this book.

LXX A (Codex Alexandrinus) is dated to the 5th century. It is currently located at the British Library (Royal 1 D. VIII) in London.

LXX B (Codex Vaticanus) is dated to the 4th century. It is currently located at the Vatican Library (Gr. 1209) in Vatican City.

LXX S (Codex Sinaiticus) is dated to the 4th century. Sections are currently located at the British Library (Add. 43725) in London, Leipzig University (Gr. 1) in Leipzig, the National Library of Russia (Gr. 2; Gr. 259; Gr. 843; Fonds. d. Ges. f. alte Lit., Oct 156) in St. Petersburg, and Saint Catherine's Monastery (Neus Slg. MΓ 1) on Mount Sinai.

LXX V (Codex Venetus) is dated to the 8th century. It is currently located at the Marciana Library (Gr. 1) in Venice.

LXX 44 is dated to the 15th century. It is currently located at the Stadtbibliothek (A 1) in Zittau.

LXX 46 is dated to the 15th century. It is currently located at the National Library of France (Coisl. Gr. 4) in Paris.

LXX 58 is dated to the 11th century. It is currently located at the Vatican Library (Regin. Gr. 10) in Vatican City.

LXX 64 is dated to the 10th century. It is currently located at the National Library of France (Gr. 2) in Paris.

LXX 71 is dated to the 13th century. It is currently located at the National Library of France (Coisl. Gr. 1) in Paris.

LXX 74 is dated to the 13th century. It is currently located at the Laurentian Library (S. Marco 700) in Florence.

LXX 76 is dated to the 13th century. It is currently located at National Library of France (Coisl. Gr. 4) in Paris.

LXX 98 is dated to the 13th century. It is currently located at the Royal Library (Σ-II-19) in El Escorial.

LXX 106 is dated to the 14th century. It is currently located at the Biblioteca Comunale Ariostea (187 I-III) in Ferrara.

LXX 107 is dated to 1334. It is currently located at the Biblioteca Comunale Ariostea (188 I) in Ferrara.

LXX 122 is dated to the 15th century. It is currently located at the Biblioteca Marciana (Gr. 6) in Venice.

LXX 126 is dated to the 1475. It is currently located at the State Historical Museum (Gr. 19) in Moscow.

LXX 130 is dated to the 12th or 13th centuries. It is currently located at the Austrian National Library (Theol. Gr. 23) in Vienna.

LXX 236 is dated to the 11th century. It is currently located at the Vatican Library (Vat. Gr. 331) in Vatican City.

LXX 248 is dated to the 13th century. It is currently located at the Vatican Library (Vat. Gr. 346) in Vatican City.

LXX 249 is dated to the 13th century. It is currently located at the Vatican Library (Pii. II Gr. 1) in Vatican City.

LXX 314 is dated to the 13th century. It is currently located at the National Library of Greece (44) in Athens.

LXX 318 is dated to the 10th or 11th centuries. It is currently located at the Vatopedi (598) on Mount Athos.

LXX 319 is dated to 1021. It is currently located at the Vatopedi (600) on Mount Athos.

LXX 392 is dated to the 10th century. It is currently located at the Abbey of Saint Mary of Grottaferrata (A. γ. I) in Grottaferrata.

LXX 402 is dated to the 14th century. It is currently located at the Patriarchal Library (Σάβα 105) in Jerusalem.

LXX 538 is dated to the 12th century. It is currently located at the National Library of France (Coisl. Gr. 191) in Paris.

LXX 542 is dated to the 9th century. It is currently located at the National Library of France (Gr. 10) in Paris.

LXX 583 is dated to the 14th century. It is currently located at the National Library of France (Gr. 1087) in Paris.

LXX 670 is dated to the 14th century. It is currently located at the Vatican Library (Vat. Gr. 335) in Vatican City.

Alternative Translations

The following is a list of alternative translations that were used for comparative analysis. Both the Peshitta and Coptic translations are believed to have been heavily based on the Septuagint, although do inherit relics of older Imperial Aramaic translations, or imports from the Hebrew translation.

The Peshitta is the Syriac translation of the Christian bible. The Old Testament was translated from older Aramaic and Hebrew sources during the late-2nd century AD.

The Sahidic manuscripts are translations of the Septuagint into Sahidic (also known as Thebaic), one of the six dialects of Coptic, the classical era form of the Egyptian language. Sahidic was the dominant form of Coptic used before the 11th century, and is believed to have originated in the region around Hermopolis, at the boundary between Upper and Lower Egypt. Translations of the Septuagint into Sahidic are known to have existed by the 4th century, however, early non-dialect specific translations are generally accepted as having been made as early as the 1st century AD, with some scholars suggesting the 1st century BC. The early non-dialect specific forms of Coptic are generally grouped with Sahidic, as Sahidic did not have a standardized spelling until the 6th century.

The Armenian bible was translated from the Septuagint in the 5th century, replacing the older Armenian bible that had been translated from Aramaic texts, however, includes some of the older names.

The Ge'ez manuscripts are Classical Ethiopic translations of various ancient Israel books that comprise the Christian bible, Jewish Tanakh, and Beta Israeli Orit. They were sources from texts in multiple languages, including Coptic, Greek, Aramaic, and Arabic.

ALTERNATIVE TRANSLATIONS

The Vetus Latina are the old Latin translations of the Septuagint and other Israelite texts that predate Jerome's Latin Orthodox Bible in the 5th century. Some of the texts appear to have been translated directly from Aramaic or Hebrew source texts, however, most appear to have been translations from the Greek translations. The version of Tobit found in the Vetus Latina manuscripts is far closer to the Codex Sinaiticus' version of Esther than the more common versions found in Septuagint manuscripts, suggesting it was translated from an Aramaic source.

Codex Sangermanensis 4 (VL 7) is a copy of the book of Tobit which dates to 825. It is currently located at the National Library of France (Fonds lat. 11553), in Paris.

Codex Complutensis 1 (VL 109) is a copy of the book of Tobit which dates to 850. It is currently located at Complutense University Library, in Madrid.

The Codex Monacensis (VL 130) is a copy of the books of Tobit, Judith, and Esther which dates to 800. It is currently located at the Bavarian State Library (Clm 6239), in Munich.

The Codex Bobbiensis (VL 135) is a copy of the books of Tobit, Esther, and Maccabees which dates to 875. It is currently located at the Biblioteca Ambrosiana (E.26), in Milan.

The Codex Regius (VL 148) is a copy of the book of Tobit that dates to 850. It is currently located at the National Library of France (Fonds lat. 93), in Paris.

ALTERNATIVE TRANSLATIONS

The Codex Corbeiensis (VL 150) is a copy of the book of Tobit which dates to 822. It is currently located at the National Library of France (Fonds lat. 11505), in Paris.

Available in Print

AVAILABLE IN PRINT